C000050123

MICHA

Michael Grist is the British/American author of the bestselling Chris Wren thrillers, writing as Mike Grist. Born and brought up in the UK, he has lived and worked in the USA, Japan and Korea, and currently lives in London.

He has been a teacher, photographer and adventurer. His photography of abandoned places draws millions of visitors to his website. He also writes science fiction and fantasy novels under the name Michael John Grist.

www.michaeljohngrist.com

Christopher Wren Thrillers (writing as Mike Grist)

1. Saint Justice

2. No Mercy

3. Make Them Pay

4. False Flag

5. Firestorm

6. Enemy of the People

7. Backlash (upcoming)

Last Mayor Apocalypse Thrillers (writing as Michael John Grist)

1. The Last

2. The Lost

3. The Least

4. The Loss

5. The List

MASTER YOUR GENRE

HOW TO MEET READER EXPECTATIONS AND SELL MORE BOOKS

MICHAEL GRIST

SHOTGUN
BOOKS

SHOTGUN BOOKS

www.shotgunbooks.com

Copyright © Michael Grist 2021

ISBN: 978-1-7399511-0-8

CONTENTS

I. GENRE MASTERY

MORE WRITERS than ever before dream of getting their work into the hands of readers. Some are succeeding; reaching wide readerships, making enough to become full-time authors and even earning six- or seven-figure incomes at the top of the bestseller charts. Others may spend thousands on editors, ads courses and marketing packages only to come up repeatedly in the red, struggling to sell even a book a month.

Why is this happening?

The answer is Genre Mastery.

Successful authors listen to their readers at every chance they get. They seek out new ways to satisfy and delight those readers, all while getting across their own creativity, ideas and message without compromising their core vision. They understand that books can evolve - that is, books can be changed, adapted and improved in real time, inspired and informed by reader expectation.

I know because I've been on both sides of this equation.

My name's Michael Grist, and I've written and published 23 books across multiple Genres, including Fantasy, Science Fiction, Travel Guide and Thriller. With many of those books

I struggled to reach readers, either losing money or breaking even - until I started seeking out and listening to reader feedback using a range of simple new techniques.

Over the course of several years I developed and implemented these techniques, and as a result saw my backlist sales improve gradually until they finally hit a turning point in March 2021 with my 'Christopher Wren' Thriller series.

My readership rocketed overnight. Suddenly I was selling hundreds of copies a day. Where before people had stopped reading at book 1, now they were tearing through all 5 books within days. My income transformed. Within a few days I was making enough to replace my job, then enough to double it, then I hit six-figure author status.

I could hardly believe it. This was my childhood dream - to reach readers the same way my favorite authors had reached out to me. At first I thought these sales were going to be a flash in the pan, but they kept on going. Ads that hadn't worked before suddenly did. Reviews improved. Sales kept climbing. Readers were loving the books and telling their friends.

I'd mastered my Genre.

You can too. This book is going to show you how: to reach more readers, sell more books, maybe make a living from your own creative ideas and even hit bestsellerdom, without any formulas or set-in-stone Genre templates.

You'll master your Genre. Let's get started.

Genre & Readers

To achieve Genre Mastery, we have to talk about what Genre means to readers.

Genre is a term often used dismissively, but at its core it

just means a type or category of writing, with a particular content, style and form, that provides a specific emotional or informational reader journey.

In that sense, almost every piece of writing fits into one Genre or another. Look at the top 100 bestseller charts on any given day and they'll be crammed with a huge variety of Genres, from Thriller, Romance, Science Fiction and Literary to History, Business, Cookery and Autobiography.

All of these Genres provide their own distinctive reader journeys, whether that's the emotional and intellectual heft of a Literary novel, the rollercoaster excitement of a Thriller, the uplifting love of a Romance or the instructive steps of a How-To Guide.

We're all familiar with these kinds of Genres. Thrillers have fights, Romance has love, How-To Guides have infographics, and so on.

But there's more to it than that.

Within each Genre are many subGenres, each with their own flavor of content, style and form. For example, Vigilante Justice is a subGenre of Thriller featuring a lone vigilante in the modern world (like Lee Child's Jack Reacher), who rolls into town and sets an injustice to rights. This is pretty similar to the Western, either another Thriller subGenre or a whole Genre to itself (depending on whom you ask), where the same kind of thing happens, but set in the Wild West era, with horses, saloons and cattle rustlers.

Similar but different.

Likewise Paranormal is a subGenre of Romance, where a young woman falls in love with magical beings (such as vampires and werewolves in the Twilight books), often ending with a magical fight of good against evil. Compare that to the Billionaire Romance subGenre, where a young woman falls in love with a billionaire playboy, perhaps even with erotic elements like in Fifty Shades of Grey. There are similarities across these subGenres (Fifty Shades famously began life as Twilight fan-fiction), but it's the differences that are important.

Even Literary fiction has subGenres, or serves as a subGenre to other Genres (again, depending on the person doing the categorizing). Margaret Atwood's 'The Handmaid's Tale' is Literary Dystopian Science Fiction, which puts it in the same overall Genre as 'The Hunger Games'. 'Where the Crawdads Sing' is a Literary Mystery, in the same overall Genre as Agatha Christie books, but layered with narrative complexity and rich worldbuilding.

These subGenres overlap everywhere. They are constantly shifting, as the culture changes to reflect reader tastes. Some subGenres fade in popularity while new subGenres surge up and old subGenres blend in fascinating new ways. This is one reason why there can be no authoritative list of Genre conventions. It is these overlapping, constantly shifting subGenres, and the readers who love them, that make writing and reading so exciting, and also that propel the bestseller charts.

These readers know exactly what kind of journey they're looking for in a book, and seek it out like a homing missile. They *are* the bulk of the book market, and that market's new gatekeepers. Make it with them and you can cross over into the mainstream - but to achieve that you've got to satisfy their expectations, though that does not mean slavishly following a strict list of Genre restrictions.

If anything, readers are looking for two things; a certain amount of their expectations to be satisfied, *combined* with a substantial helping of delight from story ideas that are fresh and original. Your ideas. Your vision. Combining these story ingredients successfully boils down to aligning three key steps in the reader journey:

- Genre
- Promise
- Delivery

Genre

Genre and subGenre readers (henceforth I'll use the terms somewhat interchangeably) know what kind of emotional or informational journey they're looking for in a book, because they've taken that journey many times before. Whether it's an uplifting Cozy Romance, a heart-pounding Terrorism Thriller or a hard-charging Business Self-Help Guide, they know exactly how to recognize their preferred subGenre by its packaging Promise: the cover, title and blurb (back cover/sales page text).

Promise

A book's cover, title and blurb make a Promise to readers, saying 'this experience will be similar to that experience you had before, so you're going to enjoy it too.' This makes an obvious kind of sense. If you've written a book about young wizards going to school, it should look something like Harry Potter, so readers will know what they're in for.

Success here requires that your Promise (your cover, title and blurb) aligns with your target Genre (maybe 'Wizards and Witches Fantasy' or 'Coming of Age Fantasy'). It absolutely shouldn't be a carbon copy of Harry Potter, but if you can hit enough reader expectations, you'll earn a greater readership.

Failure comes when your Genre and Promise don't align,

and your book looks and sounds nothing like other books in the subGenre. The reader's looking for something similar-to-but-different-from Harry Potter, and either your cover, title or blurb doesn't signal that, so they'll move on down the line.

We want them to stop and pay attention to your book. We want to give them something familiar enough that they'll give your book a second look, after which they'll dig into your body text (the book itself) and be delighted by all the unique ideas and creativity embedded in your story.

But the work isn't done when we align our Promise (the cover, title and blurb) to our Genre. Promising the reader something they want will help you sell a single book, but to build an author career you need to Deliver on that Promise.

Delivery

Delivery means providing a body text that largely aligns with both your Genre and your Promise, thereby satisfying your reader's expectations. Do that, and you'll get repeat customers - readers who are hungry for your next book. But if the body text doesn't sufficiently align to your Promise or Genre, whether in characters, settings, tropes, themes, language, plot or whatever, you won't be getting those return readers.

Again, this makes sense. If I as a reader go out looking for a Regency Romance, find one that looks incredible based on a sumptuous cover, delicious blurb and engrossing title, then find the body text to be 'Pride and Prejudice and Zombies' (a real Genre mash-up book) I'm unlikely to be happy. I won't go on to read another next book by this author (maybe 'Abraham Lincoln Vampire Hunter?').

Success here results in great reviews, strong sales of your backlist and future titles along with an engaged, evangelizing fan community. Failure results in bad reviews, poor backlist and future sales and a potential fan lost.

Writing as Tenpin Bowling

To help illustrate the way Genre and subGenre work, imagine the writer as tenpin bowler.

The goal for all bowlers is to hit a strike at the end of the lane - let's consider that satisfying your reader's expectations. Ultimately, every strike looks the same on the scoreboard. A good score, a satisfied reader. But no two bowlers bowl exactly alike. There are in fact many, many ways to bowl a ball down that lane. Bullet fast balls. Curving spin balls. Slow sweepers that tumble the pins with aching precision. That creative variation provides the excitement in bowling, and the delight in reading that readers also crave. Something new, dramatic and exciting - while still scoring a satisfying strike.

Satisfy the reader = give them enough of what they already want.

Delight the reader = give them something they've never seen before.

To fully win a new reader as a fan, we have to do both. But here's the rub. It's impossible to get a strike if you disregard the gutters either side of your lane.

Those gutters are the borderline of any given subGenre. Not so tight and prescriptive that there isn't enormous room for fresh new techniques within them. But ignore the gutters completely, either because you don't care about them or you don't realize they are there, and that's where your ball, or your book, will end up.

Recycling back through the machinery to pop up by your side, ready for you to bowl again. But when you bowl again (write your next book), and still disregard the gutters, or even (heaven have mercy!) go sideways to bowl in a completely different lane, the same thing's going to happen. It'll keep happening until you make some effort to bowl according to expectation, by aligning your Genre to your Promise to your Delivery.

Here's a simple graph showing how a loosely aligned reader journey would look, expressed across a spectrum of thriller subGenres (or multiple 'lanes'), such as Vigilante Justice, Serial Killer, Terrorism and so on. In this case let's say we're targeting readers of Psychological Thrillers (something like 'The Girl on the Train'); that's our lane:

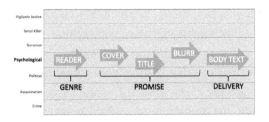

As you can see, everything here is aligned mostly within the same lane. We're doing our own thing with the story while also staying out of the gutters, providing a mostly harmonious, but fresh and original, reader journey right toward the pins. Readers went looking for that Psychological Thriller and mostly found it in the Promise of your cover, title and blurb, then were mostly Delivered it in your body text.

Satisfaction meets delight.

Beautiful.

Of course, this close alignment doesn't mean your book is a clone of 'The Girl on the Train'. Far from it. We're just bowling on the same lane as Paula Hawkins (that book's author). The way we bowl should and will be different. Our only goal here is to stay in the lane of our readers' expectations and score a strike at the end.

Now, mastering our own unique way of bowling (delighting the readers with our original ideas) while also staying out of the gutter and hitting a strike (aligning to expectation and satisfying the reader) is not easy. Even if you see and respect the Genre gutters, it's creatively challenging to do both.

Here is what many writers often produce instead:

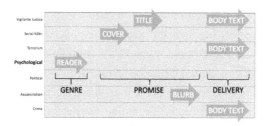

We start with the same reader seeking a Psychological Thriller, but now our book's way off lane. We're offering no alignment or consistency in our Promise or Delivery. We think we're targeting Psychological Thrillers, but our cover says Serial Killer (imagine 'The Silence of the Lambs'), our title says Vigilante Justice (Jack Reacher again, or even 'Rambo'), the blurb is Assassination (picture 'John Wick'), and the body text is some melting pot of three different subGenres.

We're miles away.

All these subGenres are different lanes with different expectations. By bowling on the wrong lanes, we're neither satisfying nor delighting our readers. Imagine turning up to watch the World Tenpin Bowling Championships, and everyone's switching lanes at random, tossing balls right down the gutter then cheering like it was a strike, even some trying to throw balls at other players, straight up through the ceiling or into the Space Invader arcades.

Wacky, yes. Entertaining in a way. But not tenpin bowling, and not what you've come there to see.

I see this all the time - authors sending balls that are not getting strikes or even troubling any of the pins, because the author either doesn't know or doesn't care about the gutters, the lanes or readers' expectations. I've done this plenty of times myself. I have three Cyberpunk thrillers that I can't get into readers' hands no matter how hard I work on my Promise and Delivery, because the problem is baked right into the body texts: these books impossibly straddle multiple Genre lanes, and that cannot easily be resolved.

This is the reason we're not all reaching readers the way we hope to - we don't align our works enough to reader expectation. These books may be beautiful, wondrous, clever, earth-shaking, but they won't easily fit into any Genre alignment, and few readers are going to experience their beauty and wonder. They don't tap into preconceived expectations of what readers want, and without those expectations on our side, we're battling a hurricane.

Here's a fun writer's lament:

"Alas, if only readers came to my work unburdened by expectation!"

Of course, readers do have expectations. They have a lifetime of them, and there's no stopping that. They've come to see tenpin bowling, not wrestling, or opera, or the pogo stick Olympics. You could choose to battle these expectations and try to push your own path through the hurricane from the outset (indeed an admirable but incredibly difficult quest), or you could start putting up sails - maybe just a single small one, maybe many large ones - and take your shot at riding that hurricane wind toward the readership you've always dreamed of.

OK. So, how?

Key Points

- Mastering Genre is key to reaching more readers.
- To Master Genre, we have to align our Genre, Promise (cover, title, blurb), and Delivery (body text).
- Genre Mastery does not mean repetitive writing to a strict formula. It means staying within your bowling lane so you can hit a strike (satisfy the reader), while bowling in your own creative, original way (delight the reader).

II. RIDE THE HURRICANE

When I started searching for the key to harness Genre readers' expectations, with my backlist of 23 titles that had landed variously off- and between-lanes, I had one key piece of advice to guide me.

Write to market.

This advice stems from the excellent book on the subject by Chris Fox, and it means identifying the space where what you want to write overlaps with what readers want to read. Some have called it 'trend-chasing' over the years, as in rushing to copy whatever book recently hit the top of the charts, but that's not at all what it means to me.

Write to market can best be expressed in a diagram:

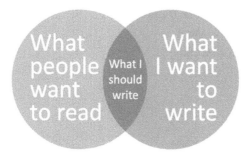

As you write to market, you're not writing something you hate just because it's popular and you're looking for a fast pay day. You're looking at what you love, and at what readers love, and finding the tenpin bowling lanes where those two fields overlap.

That's beautiful, in a way. I write what I want. The reader gets what they want. We meet in a happy middle ground.

This advice got me started down the path to reaching more readers, a search that led me to create the Genre Mastery Cycle, which in turn led to my thrillers taking off and finding more readers than I'd ever expected.

The Genre Mastery Cycle is a proven 3-stage process you can go through in any order, skipping where you want, repeating where you need to, for just about as long as you like, always learning different things about your Genre and your work that spark revelations in other areas. You might only use one technique ever and see some benefit, or use many and become a bestseller. Either way, the ultimate goal is to start a virtuous circle turning that should lead to more readers and better revelations, the longer and faster it spins.

Here I'll outline the Cycle's three stages in broad strokes, before digging into the actual techniques you can use in the following chapters:

1. **Research & Define**
2. **Ask & Align**
3. **Sell & Refine**

1. Research & Define

Research is your foundation for everything that follows, and involves analyzing the top 100 covers, titles, blurbs and body texts of comparable authors in your Genre. As you Research, using any of a range of simple analytical tools, you're going to be constantly thinking about where your book fits best - defining your target subGenre.

The benefit of the Research stage is it's great for covering known unknowns - e.g., you know that you don't know enough about what covers in your Genre look like, but you also know how to remedy that: go and look at them.

The limitation with the Research stage is that it won't help you with unknown unknowns. The things you have a blind spot for, like not realizing covers in your Genre have very specific colors, even after studying those covers yourself. This happens all the time, and we all have such blind spots. It happened to me with the first covers for my Epic Fantasy series - this subGenre often has a figure standing in the center, wielding a sword or axe and looking out at a dragon or some epic scenery. My cover had a face in full close-up and nothing else, so I didn't send the right signal to my readers.

To get to grips with these blind spots, we need to actively seek out the wisdom of others and Ask:

2. Ask & Align

Once you've got a cover, a title, a blurb, the body text or some combination of all four for your book, it's time to throw open the doors and Ask other people to weigh in. These other people could be other authors, experts like editors and cover designers, beta readers or the masses, with many different ways to get their opinions. Once you have their input, you can consider whether and how far you want to align your book to their Genre expectations.

The benefit of the Ask stage is that it will uncover the blind spots that your Research couldn't uncover, and guide you in further aligning your Promise and Delivery to your Genre expectations.

The main drawback of the Ask stage is the cost and time it takes to get opinions from other people: if you use top editors and cover designers, it can run into the thousands and take many months. A further drawback is that many of the people you ask may not be your actual target readers. There's only one way to target them directly:

3. Sell & Refine

After Researching and Asking, it's time for the ultimate experiment: put your book up to Sell and use several tools to analyze the results. When you Sell, you're asking your actual target readers to vote on your Genre, Promise and Delivery via their purchase behavior and reviews. If you can't reach them the way you want during this stage, you may wish to further refine your Genre alignment.

A strength of the Sell stage is that you're getting the most genuine feedback possible from actual target readers. Is your Promise pulling them in? Is your Delivery both satisfying and delighting them, then carrying them forward to your next book or your backlist? You'll get those answers in this stage.

The weakness of the Sell stage is that it'll cost you money to run your experiments. In order to find out if your newly aligned book works, you'll have to send people to your book's sales page, whether that's through ads or a discount newsletter promotion.

Spin Up a Virtuous Circle

As you move through the Genre Mastery Cycle, issues of alignment that you don't understand or fully agree with are very likely to rise up. Some of these issues you may wish to disregard, others you may want to dig deeper into, and this could spur you to plunge back around the Cycle seeking even great revelations.

This can be a wonderful thing. I call it spinning up a 'virtuous circle' - a concept created by legendary business guru Jim Collins. A virtuous circle describes a system that constantly picks up momentum and self-improves the longer it runs, which is exactly how the Genre Master Cycle works. The more data you feed it, whether that's through Researching, Asking or Selling, the faster and better it turns. Collins calls this spinning up your 'flywheel'.

I've been around the Cycle countless times for all my books, but none more so than for my thrillers. Many is the hour I've spent looking at comparable author covers in multiple top 100 charts, which led to a change in blurb, which helped a note from a beta reader suddenly make sense, which chimed with a few reviews I was getting, which linked to a Genre report I'd read, which led me to better define my target Genre, and then change the body text and the tagline to align, then sell more and get more focused reviews as a result, with new problems getting highlighted that previously were buried by other problems, which sent me back to asking fellow authors or beta readers, spinning through the Cycle faster all the time.

In this sense, the Genre Mastery Cycle is a prime example of an *iterative* process - one that improves cumulatively over time. Just as Apple produces a new and improved version of its iPhone every year, building on the strengths of the last iteration while also fixing any problems, we can do the same with our books.

This can be fun and heady stuff. Revelations can come thick and fast, not just about your Genre and your book, but about your readers and even yourself. I know I've learned a great deal about all of these through the Cycle.

Start by taking one small step closer to your readers. They'll come one step closer to you. You'll get into a virtuous circle together.

One Step at a Time

As you go through this book and consider the techniques it puts forth, you may at times feel overwhelmed by the large number of things you could possibly be doing. I'd like to set your mind at rest going forward: you don't need to do all of the techniques.

You don't even need to do any of them. They're tools I trialed over a period of years, and I've never used all of them for any one book.

It may be that just by reading through the Genre Mastery Cycle and thinking about your own work through the prism it provides, unexpected revelations will shake loose that could improve your book's performance with minimal effort. It could be something as simple as changing your price, taking one word out of your blurb or making the tiniest tweak to your cover.

So, read without pressure. If you'd like to, perhaps try one of the faster, cheaper or more relevant techniques, and see how it feels. All of the techniques have that information right in their headers:

- Which element each technique focuses on, either cover, title, blurb, body text, or some mixture of the four.
- Whether that technique can only be used post-publication, or also pre-publication (useful if you want to submit to agents).

- The cost required.
- The time required.

There are also lists in part V of the book with all the techniques organized by these criteria, as a convenient reference.

Generally though, I'd suggest you start easy by researching and defining your Genre. Cycle onto aligning your blurb if you like, even the title and cover if you want to, or don't. Changing your body text is the big one, something many people may never want to alter, and that's OK too. You decide how far you want to go on this crazy Genre Mastery journey.

Let's get started.

Key Points

- Mastering your Genre grew out of a Write to Market approach.
- Write to Market is not chasing after trends - it's writing both what you want to write and what readers want to read.
- The Genre Mastery Cycle is a proven process with three stages: Research & Define; Ask & Align; Sell & Refine.
- You can align to Genre as much or as little as you wish.
- Once you start working the Genre Mastery Cycle, you can spin up a virtuous circle that'll keep iterating faster the longer you feed it.
- Read through the Cycle with the pressure off - you

don't have to do all of this, you don't even have to do any of it. Try the techniques you like, if you like, in your own time.

1

RESEARCH & DEFINE

RESEARCH LIES at the core of the Genre Mastery Cycle, because ultimately this whole thing is about you gaining knowledge, and via that knowledge, defining your Genre, then aligning yaour Promise and Delivery to match it. Without Research, you'll be spraying wasted money on covers, editors and ads until the cows come home, or you happen to hit it lucky.

But hitting it lucky is not mastery. Luck is not something you'll be able to replicate, if you don't know where it came from.

This stage revolves around Research of the top 100 charts for your Genre, looking at both Promise (covers, titles, blurbs and price) and Delivery (body text) of comparable books, then trying to closely define what your Genre's features are.

It's quite possible you're currently targeting the wrong Genre, with lots of off-Genre features embedded in your work, leading to poor alignment.

What are off-Genre features? Most generally, they're whatever the readers in that Genre say they are. An example of an off-Genre feature would be including Magical Realism elements in a Cozy Romance. Cozy Romance is a subGenre of Romance without much steam, often with some comic elements. Think 'Bridget Jones' Diary'. Magical Realism is just not a part of the Genre, so readers who came to this book looking for Cozy Romance would largely be disappointed to find the magical elements.

This is a real challenge my wife and I faced as we looked to package and market her first novel. She'd written from the heart, without thinking too much about what the readers wanted. It was an excellent book that I loved, but I am not her target reader, and the Magical Realism elements she'd included made reaching her subGenre readers difficult. She lost money trying to put this book into their hands, because it wasn't what they wanted, all because we didn't know the subGenre deeply enough.

It's OK. We all do this.

The Research stage aims to start fixing this misalignment by defining your best Genre as a foundation. How do we define our best Genre? We'll get to that in more detail at the end of this stage, but it's something you'll be thinking about constantly throughout the Cycle at large. Genres and subGenres are fluid and change all the time, according to reader taste. New subGenres rise up and old ones lose their popularity - further reinforcing the idea that there are no set-in-stone 'rules' for mastering Genre, because Genre is always evolving.

That's what makes it so exciting. Essentially, you aim to learn as much as you can and take your best shot. If it turns out you're off-Genre, your readers will correct you in the later stages, as long as you keep listening. With that relationship growing, and your understanding of the shifting subGenre sands getting firmer, everything you do going forward on your Promise and Delivery will more closely align to reader expectation.

STUDY TOP 100 COMPARABLE COVERS

COVER PRE- / POST-PUBLICATION $0 10 MINS - 5 HOURS

STUDYING the top 100 for covers is as simple as it sounds, and you could spend anything from 10 mins to 10 hours (or more, over time) working on it. You'll begin with some idea of what target Genre your book falls into, though you may not be 100% certain you have it right. That's fine, we all have to start somewhere.

To start moving forward, you go to Amazon (or any other shop site), get into the bestseller charts (for Amazon go to www.amazon.com/Best-Sellers/zgbs and click either Books or Kindle Store in the left navigation table), and have a look at the various categories close to yours (read as subGenres).

There are hundreds of top 100 category lists on Amazon, sliced in ways you might not expect. Your first goal here is to look at as many as you can stomach (the charts can be overwhelming - a firehose of shapes, colors and information) and try to take it in and start making sense of it. You can see cover, title and blurb right there, and you can get a taste of the body text by clicking the Look Inside (on Amazon, at least) to read the first 5-10%.

In any given top 100, there'll be a wide range of covers.

Your goal is to start getting a feel for the types of covers that predominate. Think about colors, fonts, layout, contrast, style, image:

- **Colors.** What are the predominant colors, and color combinations? How many colors are used? Are any covers monochrome? Are the shades dark or light? Does the background match the font color or clash? I can tell you some examples from experience - Zombie books (a subGenre of Post-Apocalypse Science Fiction) are usually fiery red or muddy brown, to signify the violence and chaos of the end times. By contrast, EMP books (another subGenre of Post-Apocalypse, which stands for Electro-Magnetic Pulse, which means all the electricity in the country suddenly stops working) are uniformly grayscale, to signify the lights all going out.
- **Fonts.** Are they big or small? Are they serif (with extra little flourish bits, like Times New Roman) or sans-serif (like Arial)? Are they chunky or swirly? Does the main title font match the author's name font, or is it different? Do the fonts have effects overlaid, like a grunge filter for Zombies, or are they sparkly, like a Rom-com? You may already know that more Literary books tend to have the title font as the main event - often with graphical elements peeking out over the top. Thrillers often have a very large size of font for the author's name, even if they're not a well-known author.
- **Layout.** Where are the title and author name, are they top, middle or bottom? Is there a vignetting

effect applied (i.e. the corners are made darker to 'frame' the center of the book)? Is there a literal frame around the book's edge, like a wreath of flowers or a solid block of color? Where is the action of the cover happening, top, middle or bottom? A lot of Thriller covers put all the text at the top over a troubled sky, then have a scene depicted in the bottom third. Some have a large hollowed-out silhouette of a character, within which a scene takes place, with text pushed to the top or bottom.

- **Contrast.** Is the book dark or light or both? Does the cover 'pop' - which is to say, will it stand out thanks to the contrast between darks and lights or bold colors? It's valuable to remember most readers will see your book at thumbnail size on a computer or phone screen, and may not even be able to make out the image or the text at that scale. It's important that it grabs the eye.

- **Style.** Is the cover a photo manipulation (multiple images collaged together using a tool like Photoshop by an expert designer) or some form of illustration? Is the illustration painterly (could be Epic Fantasy), or cartoonish (could be Cozy Romance), or graphic design (could be Self-Help Non-Fiction)? Are there effects applied to the image, such as glow, sparks, fluttering cherry blossoms. It's very common in Paranormal Romance, for example, to have a female figure standing against a darker setting with glowing 'magic hands' - her hands have magicky purple or green swirly effects clouding them. This is a distinctive style you'll want to match if you're in the subGenre, and avoid if you're not.

- **Image.** What image is depicted on the cover? Many authors will give their designer a very specific brief for what they want, right down to the characters' eye color. Precise details like that only matter to the author, though, not to the browsing reader. A complex scene direct from the book, showing maybe five main characters and two main rivals in a detailed setting, will just be a data jumble. Simpler, clearer, and cleaner is better, and is mostly what you'll find in the top 100.

One major proviso you need to consider when doing this, though, is that the top 100 charts are not authoritative on what a Genre is.

What that means is, nobody sifts through the charts taking out books that don't belong. For example, the Cyberpunk top 100 is filled with the more popular litRPG Genre of books - books about adventures inside video games. They're similar Genres in some ways, but totally different in others. But, litRPG doesn't have its own Genre yet on Amazon, so they put their high-ranking books into Cyberpunk, resulting in few traditionally Cyberpunk books getting to the top.

This could be misleading, if you're trying to figure out what cover to put on your cyberpunk book. Your readers, however, will unconsciously navigate these different covers with ease. Big-time readers know exactly what they're looking for and home in on it like a shark.

It's the same in any and all top 100 charts. Vigilante Justice, a thriller Genre, is filled with shirtless man chests - because that's also a subGenre of Romance without a top 100 of its own. So if you've written a Cyberpunk or a Vigilante

Justice thriller, you have to inform yourself enough to know that you don't want colorful litRPG or a man chest.

So you're looking, scrolling, absorbing. Consider taking it to the next level and get slightly analytical.

Only slightly. Start trying to group the covers you see and make a tally. Maybe take screenshots or download the covers and combine them in a collage program like Canva so you can see them all in one place at a glance.

Maybe you're in Contemporary Romance. Count how many illustrated covers there are, how many man chest, how many with a couple, how many with a house and sea view. Once you've got them grouped, look for commonalities using the criteria we discussed above. Do they have blocky fonts or loopy cursive? Do they use pink and powder blue (that's going to be a Cozy Romance of some kind, maybe comic) or darker grittier colors (that's going to be steamy with jeopardy)?

You'll also want to be looking through from the covers to the blurbs, to get a better sense of what goes with what. Remember, there's not only us trying to get our books nicely aligned. There are other people trying to do it also - some well, some poorly. Don't get confused by someone doing it badly, look in the aggregate. Group dozens of covers.

Do this for a while, across multiple top 100 charts, and you'll get a better sense for what kind of book you have, and where it belongs.

This process is exactly how I made my first cover for my first thriller. I made it myself using the free photo program Gimp, using images from www.shutterstock.com or royalty free sites, after looking at charts and covers and grouping and such. I was looking for books like Jack Reacher books, because that's what I thought I'd written, and concluded I needed a road leading into wilderness, a dark silhouette guy walking along it, some dramatic clouds, and a very particular font placement. Here's what I had for the book's first year in publication:

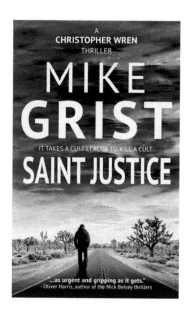

It's not perfect, but it definitely did the job of signaling Jack Reacher and appealing to Jack Reacher-expecting readers. As I went along, however, that became more of a cross to bear than a crutch, for reasons that reach across the Genre Mastery Cycle - poor reviews largely saying the body text wasn't what readers expected, with too much darkness and violence. My dark Delivery wasn't aligned to my lighter Promise.

I started thinking about how to alter the cover myself, in a way that would signal this darker content. I honestly had little idea how to do this though. I needed a little help from another form of research.

OUTSOURCE COVER RESEARCH TO K-LYTICS

OUTSOURCE COVER RESEARCH TO K-LYTICS

IF THE ABOVE analysis sounds like hard work, I'm happy to report that there's a short cut around it. A company called K-lytics produces Genre reports on the book industry, targeted at independent authors. They crunch the numbers so you don't have to, providing all kinds of metrics on various Genres.

In this way, you can outsource your Research. You can join K-lytics as a member to get a wide range of reports, or simply go to their shop page and peruse market reports per Genre for the modest price of $37 (current at time of publication - www.k-lytics.com/shop/). In these reports they have analysis of titles, Genres, covers, sales numbers, competitiveness and more.

For covers, K-lytics provide a grouping just as I recommended doing above - what percentage of books in a given Genre have man chest, for example, or use pinks and blues, or use loopy cursive text. This could be a starting place, if you find the fire hose of top 100 charts too much to grapple with. People who study the Genres for a job have already done some of the filtering work for you.

I bought the Vigilante Justice pack a year ago, and

amongst other data, paid particular attention to the cover analysis. It echoed my own research largely - that silhouette figures walking away into the wilderness was a big thing. The one thing I noticed from this analysis were two unknown unknown I hadn't noticed myself. First was how dark many of these covers were in overall tone, and second was in how many of the silhouettes were holding guns or running.

I went back to the Genre charts, and suddenly started seeing how bright and even hopeful my cover looked compared to others. My guy walking along with his hands in his pockets did not signal urgency or threat of any kind. He could be a hitchhiker or a guy out for a morning stroll. This was quite the opposite of the book's dark content.

So I started experimenting with darkening up the cover and adding threat. Here's what I came up with:

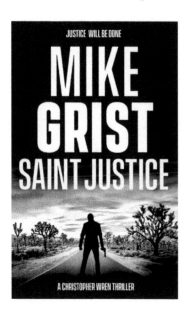

It's definitely darker. The font is blockier, similar to the books I was now seeing that I'd glossed over before. It has the guy looking angry and resolved, holding a gun. Now though the backdrop looks off, because who is he glowering at so furiously with that weapon? The desert?

Yes, well.

Did this version appeal to readers more? Maybe a little. But that wasn't really the goal. The goal was to help stem the flow a little of negative reviews from people complaining the book was too dark, when my Promise didn't match my Delivery. Now the two matched better, and I was attracting a slightly different kind of reader. You see this cover, you already know it's going to be a little dark.

So I was on track. To take things further, I was going to have to hire an expert cover designer - we'll come to that in the Ask stage. For now, let's take a look at titles.

BE INSPIRED BY COMPARABLE TITLES

TITLE PRE-/POST-PUBLICATION $0 10 MINS - 5 HOURS

AT THE SAME time you're looking at the bestseller charts for Genre cover ideas, you're going to be looking at titles too. You'll want to look at how many words are used, what kind, how they sound, whether there are nouns, verbs or adjectives. Are the nouns people, places, things? The goal is to get ideas for what works in you subGenre, as you're Cycling in on a target, while thinking about how your book could best be expressed in a similar format.

A perfect example of this process in action is my wife's first novel.

She spent years writing it, and when it came to packaging and marketing the book, I helped out. As far as Genre went, we knew it was women's fiction with some romance, but we didn't know a subGenre to place it within, and therefore didn't know what kind of cover to get, title, blurb, etc....

The book's working title was 'Hana's Bakery'. Simple and clear. The heroine is called Hana, and she starts up a bakery business. It tells us something, but at the same time it really tells us nothing. It's not a clear signal to the reader. It reports what the book is on some fundamental level, but it doesn't follow a Genre structure and it doesn't really appeal.

So we researched. We brainstormed. We scoured other Genres, looking to find what her book's subGenre was, what kind of covers they had, and what kinds of titles matched.

A few stuck out to us immediately. Definitely illustrated covers looked good, and had fun titles that felt in keeping with the tone of the book. I loved 'The Telephone Box Library', which has a beautiful village sketch with a telephone box. 'The Little Teashop in Tokyo' seemed a very close fit, as 'Hana's Bakery' is set in Tokyo. This research spiraled to finding more in this Genre, via the Amazon Also Bought strip of similar titles beneath the blurb. Many of these had titles featuring the setting heavily, really evoking a place and a mood, as well as being fun to say with repeated consonants:

- **The Corner Shop in Cockleberry Bay**
- **Autumn Skies over Ruby Falls**
- **The Cornish Confetti Agency**

I can't vouch for the quality of those books, but the titles are cute, lush, sweet and fun. That's what my wife's book is, so we needed something like that - evoke a setting, be fun and clever like 'The Telephone Box Library', as well as being fun to say like 'Cockleberry Bay' or 'Cornish Confetti Agency'.

We thought and we thought. We brainstormed. Ultimately, we came up with:

- **The Tokyo Bicycle Bakery**

It perfectly suits the book. When Hana makes her bakery, she delivers all her cakes by bicycle. It also gives the setting, Tokyo. It gave us the clear idea for the cover, and it helped reframe the whole book's body text in a way that unified it. Previously the bicycle cake delivery had just been a thing she did, not a major selling point. Reworking the book's body text a little to make it a more major point has only strengthened it.

Here's the cover:

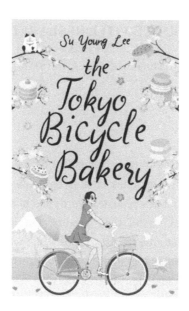

Readers have said it was both the title and the cover that drew them in. Great! That's half the job done. Drag them deeper with the blurb, and that's a sale! We got there by looking at what others in the subGenre were doing and coming up with our own take on it.

OUTSOURCE TITLE RESEARCH TO K-LYTICS

TITLE PRE-/POST-PUBLICATION $37 1 HOUR

THE K-LYTICS GENRE reports can also help when it comes to title. What the report does here is an analysis of titles and blurbs to tease out key repeated words and phrases.

I can't speak to all their reports, but in the Vigilante Justice report there was a list of most-used words/phrases, as reported by a crunching algorithm then clearly sifted through by a human, organized in several ways:

- 'Genre positioning', e.g.: Vigilante Justice, Terrorism, Assassination etc.., which must be related to category
- 'Descriptive terms', e.g.: justice, revenge, retribution, etc.., which seem to be relevant terms pulled from blurbs
- 'Crimes', e.g.: kill, murder, terror, blackmail, etc.., likewise pulled from blurbs
- 'Family ties', as above
- A word cloud of the top 100 relevant titles in the Genre

- A word cloud of the top 100 relevant blurbs in the Genre

Prior to buying this Genre research pack, I was skeptical of the value it could offer. After seeing this mathematical approach to analyzing titles, blurbs and Genres, I was totally sold.

I pored over these lists of keywords. I learned a huge amount that would go on to affect my blurb, and spur me on to produce my own larger, more targeted word clouds, as we already discovered.

First, I focused on the title information. I was very pleased, and not too surprised, to find that 'Justice' was the most-used word in the Genres, titles and blurbs of all relevant books. My thriller book 1 was already titled 'Saint Justice', so my early research had paid off there. It was bang on.

However, I was very uncertain about some of the later titles in the series. Here are the titles I had before looking at the pack:

- Saint Justice
- Monsters
- Reparation
- Release Christopher Wren

Book 2, Monsters, had always felt weak to me. It was so vague, so generic, and if anything suggested horror or fantasy. Book 3, Reparation, is a term loaded with political overtones - done consciously, as those issues are in the book, but doubtless turning a number of readers off point-blank. Book 4, Release Christopher Wren, is long, wordy, and doesn't really tell us anything. It's not propulsive, short, and macho like many titles in the Genre are.

The analysis lists really helped me pick new titles, not only by offering up in one case an actual phrase I used as a title, but in throwing another unknown unknown right in my face: my titles were off-Genre.

So I went back to look at the top 100 lists with my own eyes. I was now seeing them fresh, with some better sense of how the casual browser might see them in the store. For book 2, rather than focus on the villains with the generic 'Monsters', I decided to focus on the agency of my hero and go with 'No Mercy'. This naturally led into a new tagline, too - 'No Mercy for the Wicked'. It works nicely.

For book 3 'Reparation' I drew directly from the K-lytics analysis, adopting a term that was competitive in blurbs, meant basically the same thing as my existing title, but was more percussive and didn't have the political overtones - 'Make Them Pay'.

For book 4, 'Release Christopher Wren', I looked at competitor titles in the top 100, thought about what my audience were interested in, and started to realize things about the books I've written that I hadn't fully comprehended until that point, bouncing around the Genre Mastery Cycle.

I wasn't writing Vigilante Justice, at least not directly. Vigilante Justice normally focuses on a small threat. My books are bigger and deal with nationwide threats. After looking at more lists, and more competitors, and more analysis, I realized my books were a better fit for the Terrorism Genre. With that in mind, I went with the title 'False Flag'.

It signals perfectly. It plays into the sense of paranoia laced throughout this Genre. And it matches the story. So, from this title analysis, I further learned my Genre and better aligned my Promise. This would reflect backward on my cover, too, as when I went to get the cover done, I offered other Terrorism covers to the designer as my comparable titles.

Book 5 was then written and titled after all this deep Cycling, 'Firestorm'. It's not a popular phrase from the analytics, but it's clean, clear and signals thriller clearly. Going forward, all my titles will have to pass this test before I even write them.

CHECK COMPARABLE PRICES, FORMATS & KU STATUS

PRICE PRE-/POST-PUBLICATION $0 10 MINS - 2 HOURS

PRICE CAN BE A DECIDING factor for many readers when it comes to books in all formats, whether that's eBook, print or audiobook. It's also an incredibly easy thing for us to check - a glance at the top 100 has all the prices right there, of course depending on which bestseller chart you're in - on Amazon the Kindle (eBook) charts are different from the print charts are different from the audiobook charts, and of course all the prices are different.

As with other elements of the Promise, we'll want our prices to align with others in the Genre more widely. On Amazon, pricing for Kindle eBooks generally falls between $2.99 and $9.99, as within that range you receive 70% royalty, and outside it you receive only 30%, so you'll almost certainly want to price within the range. On other shop sites there won't be this restriction. Print book prices vary more widely - a mass print run could result in profitable $6 paperback prices, while if you're using a print-on-demand service, you'll be lucky to make a profit on anything below $10. When it comes to audiobooks, if you go through Audible or one of the other audiobook retailers, they'll typically set the price, so you won't need to worry about it.

So where within these ranges should you price? That'll come down to the expectations of your Genre. If you ask the Amazon beta pricing tool in the KDP book creation dashboard, it'll likely suggest $2.99 as your most profitable price point. But it's only a computer program, and may not know what it's talking about.

Some Genres do price $2.99 pretty exclusively. There's often a strong disconnect here between traditional publishers and independent (self-) publishers. Traditional publishers tend to price higher on eBooks, often even more than their print versions. Independent publishers tend to price lower. But those prices seem to be converging more, as independent authors realize they can charge more.

It'll all depend on your Genre expectation.

Similarly, there's the question of whether to go exclusive with Amazon and join their Kindle Unlimited (KU) subscription reading model or not. Readers of KU pay $9.99 a month to get unlimited access to a million-plus eBooks that are enrolled in the KU scheme. Authors get paid approximately half a cent per page read, and readers can 'borrow' up to 10 eBooks, magazines and in some cases audiobooks at a time. Enrolling your eBooks in KU can lead to strong income from pages read, but it also precludes you from selling those eBooks anywhere else, including your own website.

Should you enroll your books in KU, or stay 'wide' with a wider range of retailers? That's in large part a personal decision, and one that's been heavily debated across the author community. You only need to Google 'KU vs wide' to start reading up on the subject. But to some degree, it's also a Genre issue. Some Genre authors reach by far their largest number of readers through the KU program. For others, it may not be the best choice, as it cuts off access to every reader who's not buying their eBooks from Amazon.

Kindle Unlimited status is an easy thing to check - the 'kindle unlimited' branding appears perched at the top of every relevant book cover in the bestseller charts. You could make a tally of how many books in your target Genres are in KU. If it's a large proportion, bear in mind that it may be difficult to climb into those charts yourself without the added boost of KU readers. If it's a small proportion, you can more comfortably go 'wide' to other retailers at the same time as remaining on Amazon.

One example that encompasses all these issues comes from my 9-book zombie post-apocalypse series. The series started off selling quite well with book 1, but by the time all 9 books were complete my promotion efforts were no longer working, and I was losing money trying to put these books into the hands of readers.

I did my due diligence analysis, and found that readthrough across the series wasn't great. Readthrough's a simple enough concept, and means essentially what it sounds like - how many readers 'read through' to buy a second book from you after buying your first. High numbers mean readers loved the first and wanted more. Low numbers mean they didn't. There's much more about readthrough in the Sell stage.

In the case of these books, my readthrough was down to a lowly 3% by book 9. That's less than one person in thirty reading all the way through the series - a real problem. I decided to poll my newsletter fans about why they weren't reading all the way through, and one of the biggest reasons they gave was the price (amongst others - more about the other problems in the Ask stage).

For perhaps a year I'd had the eBook for book 1 priced at

99c, while every subsequent book was priced at $4.99, and most were 'wide' at multiple retailers. All told, it would cost the reader about $40 to buy all 9 books in the series. That's a really high amount, and as my fans told me, and as my own further research confirmed, extremely unusual for the Genre.

Comparable authors in the top 100 charts were charging far less, often the crazy-sounding sum of 99c for a box set of multiple books. This blew me away. How could I possible compete with my 9 books at $40 total? How were these authors making any money at all? Further research showed that all these 99c box sets were in Kindle Unlimited, which in turn meant they could sell a lot of copies at 99c, which would drive their box set up the rankings. Kindle Unlimited readers would see the box in the charts and pick it up from there, then potentially read through all the books, which would make for a hefty payday given that these were box sets often with thousands of pages.

I decided to stop trying to beat these fellow Genre authors and joined them instead. I made my 9-book series into a box set, enrolled it in KU, and with great trepidation set it at the temporary price of 99c. Here's how that looked:

I NEEDN'T HAVE WORRIED SO MUCH. With the push of a few Facebook ads behind it, the box set started climbing the Genre category rankings, and KU page reads poured in like nothing I'd seen before. Readers were reading it all the way through! A simple format, price and exclusivity change had helped bring on a windfall (though I did make some considerable other changes to align to Genre, which I'll outline later).

I kept the 99c price permanent for perhaps a year, until the page reads gradually tailed off. Maybe a few simple changes like this could transform your book's prospects, too.

WORD CLOUD ANALYSIS OF TOP 100 BLURBS

BLURB PRE-/POST-PUBLICATION $0 30 MINS

As YOU'RE PICKING out comparable books from the top 100 charts, working on both your cover and your title, you'll also be looking at the blurbs. Open up a slew of tabs in your browser and get reading. Wallow in them. Allow the words to wash over you.

Ah, refreshing.

Now let's get analytical. Coasting on feeling is not going to take us far. There will undoubtedly be certain keywords that successful authors in your target Genre are using, that a cursory glance at, or even a bath in, their blurbs will not uncover.

We can uncover them via the tool of word clouds. A word cloud is just a visual representation of word frequency from a bank of words. The words that recur the most in the bank are shown as bigger in the cloud. It's immediate, visually arresting and super clear which words are the most important.

So let's make a word cloud. The site I've been using is www.wordclouds.co.uk, but there are plenty you can find that'll do this for you for free. On that site the navigation's a little tricky, but what you'll want to do is go to the Wizard tab on the right of the navbar, select 'Type or Paste Text' (or upload a Word doc or whichever option you prefer) and input your bank of words.

From there you'll be able to experiment a little. You can change the number of words displayed via the slider. Weirdly, dragging left toward the minus symbol shows more words. Dragging right toward the plus symbol displays just the top handful of most-used words. You can also change the colors used and the shape the word cloud forms, precisely to your heart's content.

So what goes into your bank of words? You'll love this part.

You need to take all those open tabs for your target Genre books, then start copying and pasting the blurbs. It's up to you how much of the blurb you grab, whether you take the testimonial stuff and all the 5-star reviews many authors provide at the start or end, or just the actual story part of the blurb and tagline. I tend to grab it all, since it's all been selected with care, or at least it all works.

I drop that into a Word doc, so I have my own copy in case the cloud messes up somehow. You can grab ten blurbs this way, fifty, a hundred. I grabbed fifty, that's a good number, but don't feel like you have to get a huge number. It's far more important you're selecting the books that are most closely aligned to your target Genre.

Drop that word list through the Wizard into a word cloud and watch the magic happen. Instantly key words will pop out. If you've selected to include the testimonials, some of the biggest words will be author names. This is useful info. You'll want to reference these author names also in your testimonials or in the standard, 'If you like books by… you'll love this book'.

After that you'll be into nouns, verbs, adjectives. The

biggest ones here are the ones you'll definitely want to consider using in your blurb. They will not only serve as great keywords for people searching, they also clearly ring bells in peoples' minds. If they didn't, they wouldn't recur again and again. For cozy romance in my wife's Genre, it's words like uplifting, heart-warming, delicious. For thrillers in my Genre, it's your old standards like action, revenge, pulse-pounding and so on.

You might also be surprised by what you don't find here. Words you'd expected that just don't appear. This would be another unknown unknown, and it's exactly what happened to me with my thrillers.

At some point in the Genre Mastery Cycle, I came to realize my thrillers best fit into the Terrorism category. It wasn't a subGenre I'd read too much, though I'd watched plenty of TV shows (24) and movies on the topic. I figured my blurb should definitely include 'terror, terrorism, and terrorist' a few times, to make it clear.

This was also in the period when I had very violent, pretty weird content in the body text, so I was using words like 'vicious terrorists' and 'horrific scenes' and 'brutal conspiracy' and 'death cult' in the blurb. Then I did the word cloud.

I went to the Terrorism Thrillers top 100 in Amazon, opened tabs for all the appropriate-looking books, and started copy-pasting their blurbs into a Word doc. It was a lot of clicking, but only took about 10 minutes. I dropped that file into the word cloud site, and here is what popped out:

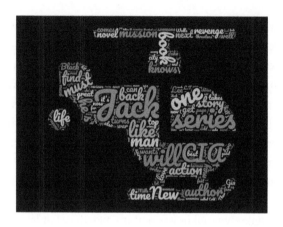

Yes, it's in the shape of a helicopter :).

Now, first thing here, we can see there are some total keywords, like Jack (for Jack Reacher, Jack Noble, Jack Bauer, any number of thriller Jacks). CIA is big. Series is big. Look closely though, and you will not find any of my words on this list.

No 'vicious terrorists', no 'horrific scenes', no 'brutal conspiracy', no 'death cult'.

'Whaaat?' I thought. So I sliced a little finer, and looked at the actual count of words appearing in the cloud. On the Wordclouds site you do this by clicking Word List in the nav bar, then you can search within the word bank and it'll give you precise frequencies for each word. Here's what I found, from the blurbs of the top 50 Terrorism thrillers on Amazon:

Vicious = 1
Horrific = 1
Brutal = 1
Conspiracy = 6
Cult = 0
Terror = 0
Terrorism = 3
Terrorist = 7

I probably don't need to tell you how completely this blew my mind. I'd fundamentally misjudged the subGenre, based on what I'd seen on TV. These top 100 books were not even using the word terror at all, even though they were about terrorism, in the Terrorism bestseller charts. There was only a smattering of 'terrorist' and terrorism'. Likewise, there was scant use of extreme words like vicious, brutal, etc....

This was one of those moments for me that resounded across the Cycle. A fellow author had once advised me to drop the use of 'brutal, vicious, etc....', and I'd listened but only half-done it. Reviews had been saying it indirectly and I'd half-absorbed it. Here it was in unavoidable black and white.

In a flash my conception of who my audience was changed completely. A lot of things fell into place. I suddenly had this idea of my readers, typically 65+ in this Genre, curling up to read one of these books before going to bed. They were looking for a little excitement, sure, but not too much. Nothing that was going to stay with them, keep them up or give them nightmares.

My books were all nightmares. I'd written the body text that way, so I was writing the blurb that way too. Obviously, here I was way out of alignment with the Genre, and as a result I made big, immediate changes. I took off all the edges of the old blurb. No more 'terror, vicious, brutal' etc.... It was still exciting, but moving toward fun and well away from horrifying.

It was a real revelation, and it came from less than thirty minutes of copy-pasting. It led to me reconsidering everything I had, what the inciting incident of the story really was, and reframing things to focus on that, something we'll look at more for the body text shortly. In brief, though, I was as surprised as anyone to discover the actual inciting incident of my story was the theft of Wren's Jeep by a biker gang.

That was it! Just the theft of his Jeep.

Lots of other things were going on at the start, many of which I thought were bigger and more important, but this Jeep theft is the act that really pulls Wren into the major plot. So, with that simple beginning finally crystalized in my mind, I wrote a new tagline for a new blurb:

'They stole his truck. Big mistake.'

It's clean, clear, and readers seem to love it. On one level, and entirely unconsciously on my part, it reminds them of the John Wick thriller movies, which is actually a great comparison. On my Facebook ads, people are always asking, 'And did they kill his dog too?' (Which, along with having his car stolen, is the inciting incident of John Wick).

Lol, I say. 'If you like John Wick, you'll love Wren'. That kind of thing. It works.

OVERWRITE TOP 100 BLURBS

BLURB PRE- / POST-PUBLICATION $0 30 MINS - 1 HOUR

A STANDARD WAY TO write a blurb is to follow some broad and generic three-paragraph blurb outline, such as:

1. **Introduce** the main character and what they want.
2. **Introduce** the main threat/obstacle blocking them from getting what they want.
3. **Introduce** stakes and hint at where things are going.

This is a powerful formula, capable of spinning up our emotions and getting us ready to click BUY in a hot second. But it's also one that breeds 'synopsis-itis' - the writer's urge to unstoppably cram in every irrelevant detail into those three paragraphs somehow, because 'the reader needs to know this'.

They don't.

One really great way to sidestep this terrible affliction and jumpstart your blurb writing is to use the blurbs of other, successful authors as models, then start a process of 'overwriting'. The experts have faced this same problem as you before, and they've figured out some formulas of their own - ways of linking words and meaning together that target reader emotions and sell books.

We can learn from them. We don't need to reinvent the wheel from scratch every time. In the words of Isaac Newton, *'If I have seen further, it is by standing on the shoulders of giants'.*

Start by copy-pasting blurbs of top comparable books that resemble yours, in your target Genre. Set each one in its own space in document, then see what it would like if you started changing nouns, verbs, adjectives and the overall structure so it reflected your story instead of theirs. This might sound like it would take a long time, but it can actually be a far faster process than writing from scratch. You're just plugging things in and shuffling sections around, after all.

This can be an amazing, transformative process. As you overwrite, you're essentially checking to see if your book's 'sizzle' - the exciting and emotional parts of your story that will draw people in - is similar to the sizzle of some other books that are already selling. It helps you avoid piling your blurb high with synopsis-itis 'steak' - all the details you think the reader needs to know which they don't.

You will be surprised at what directions this process will take you in.

Some blurbs won't match your book at all, but they'll get you thinking. Others may be a great fit. Wow, right? Make enough changes after this point, combine, rearrange, introduce your own ideas and unique elements, and soon your blurb will be totally different from any of the originals, while having its own Frankensteinian sizzle engine powering it.

It'll be unique. It'll be your book. It'll probably be your best blurb yet.

WRITE THE BLURB FIRST

BLURB PRE-/POST-PUBLICATION $0 30 MINS - 2 HOURS

IT CAN BE EXTREMELY useful to write out a blurb before you even begin writing the book. This is something I started doing after working my way through the Cycle multiple times, and finding myself wishing I'd smoothed out a few off-Genre edges before I'd written them into the plot.

Oops, too late. But it needn't be too late for the next book.

I spend an afternoon on this exercise, perhaps, though it's an iterative process that adapts as I write deeper into the book. It's kind of like planning out the plot - and I'm not a prescriptive planner, rather I'm a discovery writer with an overall vision, but I need to have a blurb and title's worth of direction before I get going, as well as a level of confidence that this is a book I'll be able to market and sell.

Is the blurb attractive? Does it have the sizzle you need to suck readers in? You could even road-test this blurb before you write word one of the book, using techniques from the Ask stage of the Cycle. You may find it's not great, and if the blurb's not great, and it's not going to help you sell the book, why write the book following that blurb?

Fix the blurb first. Make sure it's what readers want (and

what you want too, of course) before you dedicate a few hundred hours of your life to bringing it to life. It'll save you time at the end, trying to wrangle what you've written down to a few hundred words of punchy sales copy.

I recommend it also as a way to provide a kind of lodestar going forward. As I discovery write, I can sometimes get lost in the trees and lose sight of the forest. So I regularly check in with my blurb, kept always at the top of any doc I'm working on, to be sure I'm following the rough plan and Delivering on the blurb's Promise. A clear and powerful blurb can encapsulate the emotional experience you want to give your readers, and really help to keep you on track.

READ COMPARABLE BESTSELLERS

TITLE, BLURB, BODY TEXT PRE-/POST-PUBLICATION ~$4 EACH
7-10 HOURS EACH

NEXT UP, and perhaps the most obvious thing you can do, is to read widely in the Genre you're targeting. Easy to say, but if you haven't yet accurately defined your Genre, you may not know where to start. There are dozens of Thriller Genres, dozens in Romance, dozens in Fantasy and Sci-fi and so on.

After bathing in comparable authors via the Bestseller charts, you'll have a good idea what subGenre you are, so select it, pick some top sellers and start reading. You could actually read the opening chapters of as many books as you want for free via the Look Inside on Amazon if you don't want to pay, or you can buy them and read the whole thing.

What you're looking for here, and there's no real AI shortcut like there was the word clouds, is commonalities. Tropes. Events, scenes, settings, characters and themes that recur. Tone, too. You could make precise notes of these, if you wanted, chapter by chapter, or keep a running tally of similar events, or just try to keep it all in your head.

When I hit this stage in the Cycle, I thought my thrillers were primarily Vigilante Justice, so that's what I read. I started by picking 5 of the top books in the Genre and reading them through. It was actually pretty amazing to me how much commonality I found that I hadn't fully expected.

Here's a few:

- Early on there's often a 'getting kicked out of the CIA/FBI' scene, after which the hero goes rogue.
- There is typically only one point of view perspective: the hero's.
- The tone is PG-13. Lots of deaths and violence, but no gore, no swears, nothing too extreme.

Now, I wasn't following any of these tropes. But I figured I could, without losing anything of importance to the story or my message, so I started working on them. Over something like a year, fueled by further feedback from across the Cycle, I made changes to the body text that had a huge impact on sales and readthrough.

Here's a few:

- Added a 'getting kicked out of the CIA' scene. Previously my hero had quit the CIA by the time we meet him. Adding the scene in was dramatic and straightened out the narrative.
- I had multiple perspectives throughout the story, but it was actually pretty easy to cut all these completely, simplifying and speeding up the book in one fell swoop. All the important moments shown in those alternate points of view still happen, but now they happen off-camera, as experienced by my hero.
- When it came to the PG-13 issue, however, I hit a big personal blind spot. This issue chimed well

with what I was hearing from reader reviews about how dark and violent my books were, but I couldn't see it. I'm steeped in TV thrillers, which are often R-rated, so I didn't know what parts were pushing too far. I needed something to guide me.

USE MOVIE CLASSIFICATION TO DEFINE TONE

BLURB, BODY TEXT PRE-/POST-PUBLICATION $0 1-10 HOURS

IN MY HUNT for ways to grade my thrillers to a PG-13, mainstream kind of level, I came across the well-established system of movie classification. This system has clear boundaries and guidance for revising movies to get the right certificate, whether that's G, PG, PG-13 or R. For some people it's their whole job to make these decisions, establishing where the borderline between classifications lies.

As soon as I realized this, I felt like a kid in the candy store. I didn't have to flail around wondering what I'd done that was so dark - I could figure it out, and you can too, if you're concerned the content of your book is pushing out of the mainstream.

This could be in terms of violence, as in my case, but also language, steaminess, how challenging the issues are, and any number of other things for which movies are also graded. I did some web searches hunting for movie classification guidance, and stumbled upon the website of the BBFC.

That's the British Board of Film Classification. Never fear, non-Brits, I'm certain this information will still be useful for you too, even though our precise classification systems may be slightly different.

On the BBFC website there are case studies - www.bbfc. co.uk/education/case-studies - and in one afternoon I dug deep into these. I found all kinds of original case notes for top movies in multiple Genres, but the one that influenced me most was on the James Bond movie Casino Royale. This case study was a masterclass in parsing violence to know where the precise line is. I recommend you read it if you're at all interested in the subject - www.bbfc.co.uk/education/case-studies/casino-royale.

In summary, the filmmakers wanted a PG-13 and were getting an R, primarily because of a scene where Bond is being tortured. You may remember this scene - Bond is sitting naked on a wicker chair with no bottom, while the torturer swings a knotted rope into his, ahem, undercarriage. The classifiers described the changes necessary to get a PG-13 rating, things like fewer shots of the camera lingering on Bond's pained face, decreasing the intensity of the sound effects and music, dialing down the sadistic pleasure of the torturer, and focusing more on Bond's resilience, agency and his dark sense of humor in the face of the pain.

The filmmakers made those changes, and they worked. Casino Royale is a PG-13 in the US, a 12 in the UK. That rope scene is still demonstrably a torture scene, but now the edge has been taken off, the threat and realism are reduced, and we're never too afraid that Bond is going to be irrevocably damaged.

Reading these reports really shifted my thinking. I began to see where my books were too dark. With the highly logical reasoning of the BBFC's case studies in my head, I made the following changes across many months, again in concert with further feedback from across the Cycle:

- Un-kill many of the people who help Wren. Previously they all died in various horrible ways. Now few of them do, and have even gone on to play important roles in the sequels! I'm very glad I un-killed them.
- Un-kill many of the bad guys, where Wren thinks there's room for salvation.
- Un-torture everyone. There were several gruesome torture scenes before, and now they're gone. There is still torture in the background, but the camera no longer dwells on it.
- Remove almost all swearing. This is another issue of tone the classification system brought to my attention. Previously I had lots of f-bombs and other swears. Now I have only 'bullshit' and a few 'damns'.
- Remove reference to Wren using any drugs stronger than coffee and generic painkillers, as casual hard drug use gets you an R, and my hero was a bit of an addict. Now he just loves him some black coffee.

Just as with the changes I made to my tropes, these gradual shifts of tone had a beautifully gradual effect on sales, readthrough and reviews, taking place over a year until the series hit take-off. I worked the Cycle again and again, each time building up the flywheel's speed. The easy stuff came first, reducing violence and swearing. The harder stuff came later, rewrites and structure shifting. Better problems came to the fore.

Better problems still are coming to the fore. Just yesterday I got a fresh reader review that brought up some things I'd never thought of. I built changes in and republished the book on top of itself. The next iteration. So the Cycle keeps spinning and the book gets better.

READ YOUR REVIEWS

COVER, TITLE, BLURB, BODY TEXT POST-PUBLICATION $0
5 MINS

MANY AUTHORS SAY, 'Do not read your reviews', and I totally understand this advice. Reviews can be disagreeable and painful. If you take criticism to heart, as most of us do, a negative review could really set back your confidence. So take what I say with a pinch of salt, and your own wellbeing in mind:

Read your reviews.

This may be one of the most important things you can do, when it comes not only to Defining, but also to Aligning and Refining your book to Genre. In the Genre Mastery game, we're looking for as much data as we can get about what our readers really think, and there's no more direct answer to that question than the reviews they leave us.

Now, you should do your very best not to take them to heart. This may mean disregarding 1-star reviews, or getting a friend to filter them for you, at least until you have enough 5-star reviews to dilute their demotivating effect. Bear in mind that a 1-star reviewer may just reflect the wrong person getting their hands on your book. Maybe they were having a bad day and wanted to take it out on someone. You can't let their bad day spoil yours.

If you do read a 1-star review, though, and it hits like a punch, allow yourself some time reading your 5-star reviews. There may not be much in these happy reviews that you can use to fuel the Cycle, but they'll work wonders for your mental health (and your ego). I have been known to do this myself at times...

Another coping mechanism is reading the 1-star reviews of books you love. It just shows it takes all sorts. You're not alone in getting singled out for attack. You're in good company.

So what then becomes of your 2-star, 3-star and 4-star reviews? Well, you should read them. These reviewers liked something about your book, while having some problems with it too. There can be absolute gold in what they say.

I have learned so much from my reviews. I keep a close eye on them every day, looking out for anything I can use. Sometimes it's little peccadillo where I can make an easy improvement and get a quick win. Sometimes it's the cumulative effect of reviewers repeating the same thing. Here's a few examples:

- An early 1-star reviewer of my first Chris Wren thriller said I'd mixed up the name of the bad guy multiple times at the end of the book. Unfortunately, they were right! Twice I'd put 'Arrack' when it should have been 'Acker'. An editing slip that took 5 minutes to fix, with the new file uploaded and ready to go. Easy win.
- In the early days, I was getting many reviews complaining about the darkness and violence of my thrillers, which chimed with other feedback

points I was getting from across the Cycle. I worked to grade my violence down (more on how I did that shortly), and these reviews served as a useful barometer throughout that process, reducing steadily over weeks and months as I figured out more ways to reduce the violence reduced. These days I hardly ever get reviews complaining about the violence. Big win.

- I've had my share of reviews like: "Not what I expected." I've had this on my thrillers, my cyberpunk books, my zombie apocalypse books. It's a doozy, and it means you're out of alignment. The reader though they were getting one Genre, and you gave them something else. Listen to what they say, and they'll help you define where you're going and understand what you've got.

So gird your loins. Ready yourself for the punches to come. Read what your reviewers have to say, and give yourself time to reflect. Go back to your 5-stars if you need it. But if you find there's a lot of reviewers raising the same issues, or there are typos that slipped through editing, or you've misaligned your Genre without realizing it, maybe those are punches you have to take on the chin. Use them to propel you through the Cycle as you seek greater alignment.

DEFINE YOUR GENRE
COVER, TITLE, BLURB, BODY TEXT PRE-/POST-PUBLICATION
$0 CONSTANTLY

TIME TO DEFINE YOUR GENRE! This is something you will have been thinking about throughout the process so far, and honestly you should expect to keep doing this, making further alignments and refinements for as long as you keep working through the Genre Mastery Cycle.

So how do we do it?

You take your best shot, is the answer, based on the best information available to you at the time. Your new knowledge, your feeling about the book you've written or are yet-to-write, your instincts will all come together, and that's the subGenre you go with.

In the case of my thrillers, very early on I was caught on the horns of a dilemma: should I go darker toward Serial Killer or go lighter toward Vigilante Justice? In favor of Serial Killer, I had the tone of violence and twisted darkness, but I didn't have the plot or tropes. Serial Killer is usually about one cop hunting one murderer, but my story was on a larger scale - one rogue guy hunting a national cult.

That fit better into Vigilante Justice or Terrorism, but if I went all-in for those, all the blood and twisted darkness would have to go. I weighed that decision in the balance for some time, thinking about changing either my tropes or my tone to match one or the other subGenre.

Ultimately, I concluded that I couldn't change the plot or tropes to match Serial Killer without writing a whole new book, but I could change the tone and keep the story largely intact, so that's what I did.

It meant trimming plenty of things, and many of these cuts hurt. For a while, as a kind of crutch to help me through it, I included all my 'deleted scenes' as Extras at the end of the book. That lasted for a few weeks, long enough for me to realize any reader who'd enjoyed the book, then went to the Extras seeking more of the same, was going to get an unwelcome shock when they saw the dark and violent tone, and maybe decide not to read any further.

So I bid those scenes completely adieu. They are all the way gone. The book sells.

You may need to define and trim in similar ways. It will be difficult. Like me, you will have blind spots for your Genre. That's why we need to Ask some external observers to help point them out.

FURTHER RESEARCH

THERE ARE a plethora of great books, courses and podcasts that will take you deeper into some of the aspects we've covered in the Research stage. Here are a few suggestions:

- Write to Market by Chris Fox. The seminal book on writing to market, which got me started on the Genre Mastery Cycle. Chris Fox is a bestselling science fiction author.
- Mastering Amazon Descriptions by Brian D. Meeks. A great guidebook with lots of little tricks on how to write a blurb that helps sell books. Brian Meeks is a thriller writer who also offers a blurb-writing service.
- Story Engineering by Larry Brooks. This is a fantastic, powerful book for better understanding how the body text of a book should be structured to meet reader expectation. Larry Brooks is a bestselling thriller author.
- The Self Publishing Show podcast, with Mark Dawson and James Blatch. This is a truly

excellent free weekly resource from million-selling Dawson and first-time author Blatch. The catalogue of shows is hundreds deep, and includes them talking with the top minds in writing and publishing. In particular, the Book Lab episodes. Well worth many hours of your time.

- The Six Figure Authors podcast, with Lindsay Buroker, Joe Lallo and Andrea Pearson. This is another amazing free weekly podcast, with a very deep bench of expertise amongst these six-figure authors, which they share generously.

KEY POINTS

- Research covers, titles and blurbs from the Amazon top 100 bestseller lists. Bear in mind that these lists may contain off-Genre books. Get a sense for how your Genre looks and sounds.
- Use outsourced K-lytics research packs to support your own research.
- Check prices, formats and KU-status for comparable books in your Genre.
- Copy-paste top blurbs into a word cloud program to check key words you should and shouldn't be using.
- Consider the overwriting technique, modelling top-selling blurbs to construct/frame your own.
- Write the blurb first to check it has sizzle and keep your eyes on the prize.
- Read some comparable books in your Genre, tally tropes and tone in comparison to your own work. Make adjustments where necessary.
- Consider researching the BBFC movie

classification case studies to help guide your body text's tone.

- Define your Genre as best you can, and be open to refinements going forward.
- Research widely by reading the recommended books and listening to the recommended podcasts.

2

ASK & ALIGN

BY THE TIME you hit the Ask and Align stage, you've mostly defined your Genre and you've got something of the Promise and Delivery to ask about - could be any or all of the cover, title, blurb or body text. The key question now is, are they aligned to Genre expectations?

You must think they are. I've thought mine were multiple times and been varying shades of wrong. There's nothing like the cold crashing rocks of other people's opinions to scupper the dream. The great news is, few story ships are permanently wrecked. We can rebuild.

In this section you'll test the seaworthiness of your story craft. Are your seams watertight, the surfaces sanded down, the bilge fully pumped?

Unknown unknowns. So who will you ask?

Fellow authors will likely be your first port of call in this stage, and you can ask for their opinion both in person and online, via Facebook groups like 20booksto50k. Some great benefits of asking authors are the solidarity and support it provides, while also being free. The problem with asking authors is that, in many cases, they know no more than you.

Their encouragement or criticism can be the blind leading the blind, which may propel you to seek out experts.

Experts include editors and cover designers, and you're most likely going to have to pay for their informed input. They can be found on www.Reedsy.com, from a recommendation or via a simple Google search. The great benefit here is tapping into their experience - experts can certainly improve your craft, story, cover and even Genre alignment if they know their stuff. The disadvantage here is the cost and the time. The top experts can cost thousands, keep you waiting for months, and there's no guarantee they're going to make things better. If you're looking for cheaper and faster, you may look to beta readers.

The beta reader stage is my favorite and I highly recommend it. Beta readers can be hired off sites like www. Fiverr.com for less than $100 a pop, and function like amateur editors, offering their book assessment services cheaply and quickly, allowing you to hire dozens of betas for the same cost and time as one editor. This is the stuff the Genre Mastery Cycle is built on, getting a virtuous circle spinning. The weakness of beta readers is that they're keen readers, not editors, so while they can tell you how they felt about your book, they probably can't tell you how to fix it.

Last up, you can broaden your reach by asking the masses, via online polls of people you know on social media, or via outsourcing sites like www.PickFu.com, asking questions to large numbers of people you don't know. The advantage here is you could collect hundreds or thousands of items of feedback either free or cheaply, helping to steer your alignment. The disadvantage is that these answers will not be coming from your precise target readers.

Once you've asked, it's time to consider alignment, but what does that really mean?

Aligning to Genre essentially means making changes to your cover, title, blurb and body text to better match Genre expectation. Sometimes a change of blurb is enough. That would be easiest. Other times a new cover is needed, sometimes a new title, and often the body text itself has to change.

This can be a scary and unwelcome prospect to face. The book is complete and how you envisioned it. So, it's important to state here that alignment to Genre is a spectrum, with pure Art at one end and pure Commerce at the other. There's no set amount you have to align by. If you don't want to change your body text, no one's going to force you.

Here's a simple graph to help visualize that spectrum:

It looks rather like the Write to Market diagram from the intro, right? It is. Go a little way to the right along this spectrum, you'll likely have to file off a few unique edges from your Promise and Delivery, in exchange for reaching a wider readership. Go a long way, you'll file off a lot and reach a much larger readership.

Align a little way. Align a long way. Don't align at all. It's up to you.

I've battled this Art/Commerce dichotomy all my author career. I already mentioned my backlist, many of which were wholly written on the Art side. I let loose with my creativity; unaware it was going to seriously limit my ability to find readers. Even with my more-recent thrillers, which I'd set out to write with Genre in mind, I came out quite far to the left.

Aligning toward the center was a difficult process, and I did lose some of the uniqueness of those books. My thriller hero, Christopher Wren, started out stridently political. His politics turned off many of the readers I was trying to attract, so I worked to align him through the Cycle. Now he's still solidly political, but he's far less strident about it. I've gone to the middle to meet the readers where they are, and in turn reached many thousands of people with my underlying ideas that I never could have reached before. That's a tradeoff I'm happy with.

You'll make your own decisions and find your own comfort zone.

ASK A FACEBOOK GROUP ABOUT YOUR PROMISE

COVER, TITLE, BLURB PRE-/POST-PUBLICATION $0 10 MINS

ONLINE GROUPS like Facebook provide some of the best places possible to get feedback on your Genre alignment, your Promise and your Delivery, from fellow authors who, to some degree or another, know what they're talking about.

There are plenty of groups where you can post your Promise, the cover, title or blurb, and get a critique. You wouldn't post your body text, for obvious reasons:

- Mark Dawson's Self-Publishing Formula 'SPF Community'. You don't need to buy any of Mark's courses to get in this group, where people regularly share their covers, titles and blurbs then get a good number of comments/critiques. You've got a real mix of experts and beginners here. For broader Research, you can also access the fantastic 'Book Lab' sessions on Dawson's Self Publishing Show, a free weekly video and podcast. In the Book Lab, one author puts forward their low-selling book to get critiqued by a team of experts, both Promise and Delivery.

These episodes are excellent, and can be found here: www.selfpublishingformula.com/?s=book+lab

- 20booksto50k. This is the big daddy of all the indie author groups on Facebook, and you cannot simply roll up and post your book cover, blurb, or any of that. Doing so is likely to get you banned for self-promo, which you don't want. However, occasionally the group runs the incredibly helpful 'Why is my book not selling?' feature, where they name a Genre, ask you what you've done to promote your book so far, then allow you to share a link for critique. Here you'll get comments not only on cover, but on the title, blurb, pricing, advertising strategy, Look Inside and so on. They don't run this too often, but the past threads can be an absolute goldmine. I recommend you dig through the archives and read everything that the many commenters say, especially but not only in your own Genre. It'll really get you thinking in new and sharper ways, especially considering many of these authors are making millions off their writing a year. Find those threads in Learning Unit 20, here https://www.facebook.com/groups/20Booksto50k/learning_content/?filter=1382108652179785.
- Indie Cover Project. This is an unaffiliated spin-off of the 20booksto50k Facebook group, where the whole purpose is to share covers and blurbs and offer critiques. Again, a good mix of experts vs. beginners.
- Join the Facebook group connected to this book, the Indie Author Mastery group, where all we do

all day is talk about aligning your Promise and Delivery to your Genre.

- There are other Facebook groups you can hunt down, with a number of 20booksto50k spin-offs focusing on particular Genres, but the above are where you'll get the best responses.

One important note, and as aforementioned - you must approach anything you hear in one of these groups with your own brain fully switched on and as informed as possible from your own Research.

Countless are the times I have seen posts from authors asking for help with book sales, where they lead with a comment like:

I know my cover, blurb and book are great, so why are my books not selling?

The trouble there is, clearly one of those elements is not great, or the book would sell. You could put ads to it, and if readers found it appealing, they'd buy. Simple as. Often the problem with the book is glaringly obvious, if you know a little about the market and the top 100 charts and what readers are looking for.

We authors are not great at that side, though. We often write what we want, with little or no thought to what the reader wants. And even when we give it thought, we may not know enough about Genre or alignment to actually meet reader expectations. This can be seen all the time in the comments given to questions like the one above, 'why are my books not selling?'

Commenters may say that the cover actually is great, or they may suggest moving a couple of commas around in your blurb, or adding a drop shadow to your font, and that's all. And maybe they are right about the cover or the blurb in one sense. Maybe the cover is beautiful, a real piece of art, absolutely on point in showing a scene precisely as it happens in the book. Maybe the blurb is poetic, hauntingly written, could win you a Nobel for literature.

But none of that inherent 'goodness' matters if the Promise doesn't align to both the Genre and the Delivery. The most beautiful cover in the world on the wrong book won't help you sell a single copy.

So, you need to look out for this. It can be hard to know which authors know what they're talking about. Many don't, no offense to them. One quick way to check the authority of any particular commenter is to check their sales. A quick trip to Amazon will tell you if their books are popular. Do they have thousands of reviews? Are their books ranked sub-1000 in the overall store? If so, they're probably worth listening to. If not, maybe less so.

ASK A MARKETING CRITIQUE GROUP
ABOUT YOUR PROMISE

COVER, TITLE, BLURB PRE- / POST-PUBLICATION $2 / MEETUP
IN MY GROUP 1.5 HOURS

IF YOU'RE fortunate enough to belong to an independent author critique group in the real world, then asking them in person will function a lot like posting on a Facebook group. I have a group like that here in London, the London Indie Authors, and consider myself lucky to do so.

In our group, 10-20 regulars plus some newbies get together once a month and sometimes run a similar thing to the 20booksto50k 'Why aren't these books selling' session. The author provides a link to a sales page, and members can critique the cover, blurb, title and body text as seen in the Look Inside.

Each meeting is 90 minutes long, and we can fit three critique sessions in that time. The first 5 minutes of each 30-minute slot are spent studying the Promise and peeking at the Delivery through the Look Inside, then the next 20 are spent in open constructive critique. During this time, the author is silent and shouldn't be asked any questions. They take notes, while everyone else shares their thoughts on how to sell more. In the final 5 minutes, the author can give their comments and ask any questions they have.

These sessions are fantastic, and I always learn so much, whether I have a book getting critiqued or not. By analyzing the work of the other members, trying to figure out why they don't align to Genre, and then turning that into useful advice that'll help them get more sales, I feel like I'm attending a mini Masterclass every session. Even better, you get to hear the advice other members are sharing too, so they're shedding light on any blind spots I have.

I recommend either joining or forming a group like this yourself. Meeting up in person is great for community as well. You can set up a group on Facebook or www. Meetup.com easily enough (Meetup charges a small fee per month, but you can recoup this by charging a dollar per head), then you just need to pick a time and place that repeats every month, and start looking for members. You could do this by inviting any authors you already know, or by attending other meetings and inviting them to join yours.

Even better, in the current age such a group doesn't have to be geographically based at all, with tools like Zoom so readily available (Zoom charges a small fee also).

POLL PEOPLE YOU KNOW ON YOUR PROMISE

COVER, TITLE, BLURB PRE-/POST-PUBLICATION $0 10 MINS

AT SOME POINT you're going to have a couple of Promise options before you, it could be a handful of cover designs, several potential titles, maybe two different blurbs. You've sweated over these, and you just can't tell anymore which is better.

It's time to get a lot more opinions, fast, via an online poll. The most obvious way to do this is to ask everyone you know and then some, including fellow authors in whatever online groups you're a member of. Facebook has a dedicated poll tool for this purpose, but it doesn't really work for images, though you can easily use it for titles and maybe even blurbs. It'll count up all the response and give you a handy tally, though it may not be great for gathering comments next to the votes, and comments can be where the gold is.

I'd recommend you do the same for titles and blurbs as you would for covers, which is to clearly label them (A, B, C etc..), then post them up along with a little background info: what Genre you're targeting, what kind of feedback you're looking for.

These polls could be either your old vs. new

cover/title/blurb, or your three work-in-progress versions (as long as you have permission from the designer, in the case of covers - this is an easy process on 99 Designs), or your new cover versus a comparable author's work, or any combination of the above. Expert or otherwise, people love polls, and will give you a snap judgment, hopefully with a comment attached that can steer you. You'll swiftly get a sense of which the winner is.

You could run a separate poll for readers on your newsletter list, too. You could send it only to your elite-level inner-circle ARC (Advance Review Copy) readers, if you like. You could circulate it to your friends and family, or do a paid boost to your Facebook fans, or whatever you like to reach wider.

The main goal here is mass. You want a lot of people to see it. The more the merrier. An obvious problem of going for mass is whether you're focusing on the right kind of readers, but by getting big numbers (over one hundred responses, maybe) you're more likely to cancel out any particular biases while also capturing some readers of your particular Genre.

Ultimately, what you're hoping for is a clear preference. You'll have your own favorite, and you'll want them to pick it. If the crowd goes 90% for your favored version, that's a pretty good sign your alignment is on point. Not perfect, because remember, this is just the people you have access to. These are not your actual audience. They could easily be biased, or simply unaware of the Genre you're trying to signal, so going with their opinion may lead you astray.

But it's something, right? Useful info to have. Ideally, you'll want more. We want to be as scientific about this as we can be. To go one step further, we can ask the unbiased masses.

POLL THE MASSES ON YOUR PROMISE
VIA PICKFU

COVER, TITLE, BLURB PRE-/POST-PUBLICATION $50+, 1 HOUR
TO SET UP

THERE'S a great online feedback service called www. Pickfu.com where you pay the company to pose a question/poll to a designated number of people. The way it works is they have a large bank of people willing to answer questions, all kinds of questions, for a very small fee of pennies a pop. Amazon has a similar service called Mechanical Turk, which I looked into, but it seemed more complex than PickFu.

With PickFu they have membership options that may make running regular feedback questions cheaper, but they also offer feedback from 50 respondents for a single, unsubscribed $50 fee. If you want a larger sample, you pay more. It gets cheaper in bulk. Results come within minutes, although larger sample sizes may take longer. You also have control over the ages and interests of the respondents, though fine-tuning the sample precisely will cost you more.

It may be worth doing this fine-tuning to get a closer picture of what your target audience is. Of course, you may not yet know who your audience are, their ages or genders. One way to know this is to run Facebook ads using your book cover as the ad image, then wait and see who clicks it the most. Facebook allows you to check demographic data of your clicks, primarily gender and age.

From this, I know that readers of my thrillers lean toward men, generally over 55. Armed with this info, I'll pick over 55s on PickFu, as well as select the Crime/Mystery interest to fine-tune it. You'll do the same for your particular Genre. That sets our audience of respondents. Now we need to ask them a question.

Phrasing the question so you get meaningful responses is key. The last thing you'd want to ask is something very broad like, 'Is this a good cover?' or 'Would you buy this book based on this cover?'

You're not asking enough. I'd recommend a question more like this:

'What about this cover would prevent you from buying the book?' or 'Which of these 3 covers would you be most likely to buy and why?'

You can include with your question a picture - it could be your new cover, or a screenshot including all the key information (cover, title, blurb) from your sales page, or a picture of three different covers with clear labels (A, B, C) or anything, really. As long as your question is clear and probing, you'll get meaningful responses.

If some of the responses aren't meaningful, as in, a few people just say 'Yes' or 'No', you can easily report them and PickFu will get you some more.

Now, I used PickFu once, and opted to put my whole sales page screenshot in as the image, so they could read the title and blurb as well as see the cover. This is what that looked like:

Saint Justice: An explosive new thriller (Christopher Wren Book 1) Kindle Edition

by Mike Grist (Author), Michael John Grist (Author) Format: Kindle Edition

★★★★☆ · 343 ratings

Book 1 of 6: Christopher Wren Thrillers

Christopher Wren is a legendary figure feared the world over. Whispers call him a ghost, shredding evil organisations and leaving their leaders in the ground.

But he's not just a legend.

Born into a vicious doomsday group, Wren fled to master the dark skills of human manipulation just to survive. It made him the perfect weapon against terrorism - until he broke with the CIA in the midst of personal tragedy and fled into the wilderness of Utah.

There Wren stumbles on something truly dark. Hundreds of human cages hidden in the desert. A small town police department wiped out. A mass terror network intent on unleashing chaos.

Nobody else sees what's coming. Nobody except Wren.

America stands at a precipice. One spark in the powder keg could ignite the inferno. Now Wren finds himself alone in the dark, racing the spark as it falls.

★★★★★ "Addictive, intelligent, edge-of-your-seat writing - as urgent and gripping as it gets!" - Oliver Harris, bestselling thriller author

★★★★★ "Packed with fights, gun battles, chases and narrow escapes - a gripping story that will stay with you well after the last page is turned." - Mark Parragh, bestselling thriller author

Get started now on this explosive thriller series with an unforgettable hero.

My question was:

'Would you buy this thriller and why/why not? What would make you more likely to buy?'

With 50 respondents roughly in my target demographic, I got a wide range of feedback. Focused on the cover, someone said it looked standard for the Genre, which was actually great news. That was what I wanted. I didn't want to stand out. Others commented on the blurb, with one suggesting I add in a female character to better appeal to females, and several others saying it was too 'weird' with the doomsday group and generally too dark. More on that in the blurb section.

I found this poll very useful, in this case for the blurb, but also as confirmation of my cover choice.

POLL YOUR FANS ON YOUR DELIVERY

BODY TEXT POST-PUBLICATION YOUR NEWSLETTER COST +
1 HOU

WHO BETTER TO ASK ABOUT the Delivery of your books, the alignment of body text to Promise and Genre, than your actual fans? They'll probably be a little biased, since they 'are' fans who like your work, but they're also the people most engaged with it, and in my experience they'll be very happy to share their thoughts, whether positive and negative. They'll probably be delighted that you're asking their opinion.

In order to poll your fans, you'll need to have a way to contact them. One great way is to start up a reader's group on Facebook, where it'll be just you and your fans interacting. The only problem with a group like this is that Facebook owns it - they own the data and email of each of your readers, and controls your access to them. This means that you'll often have to pay (or boost posts) to actually reach this audience so they can see your poll.

Probably the best way to do this, therefore, is by keeping a newsletter list where you own the access, using a CRM (Customer Relationship Management) service like www. mailchimp.com or www.mailerlite.com.

To briefly sum up these newsletter services - you can ask

readers to sign up to your newsletter list at the beginning and end of your books, on your website, or even through special 'lead generation' ads on Facebook. Precisely how to do that is not within the purview of this book, but generally I'd recommend starting with Mail Chimp and following their tutorials. On Mail Chimp you'll also get an account that's free up to 1,000 subscribers, after which I'd recommend scaling up to the cheaper Mailer Lite.

But setting up newsletters, as well as what to put in your newsletters to fans, is a whole other matter. There are courses charging hundreds of dollars about how to do it, but a great place to learn more is the book Newsletter Ninja by Tammi Labrecque.

What we're talking about here is polling your fans directly about your Delivery.

Now, doing this takes some chutzpah. You have to be willing to admit to your fans that you and your work may not be perfect. I struggled a little to take this step the first time I did it, and the second, but the results I got were so phenomenal that I can't but recommend it.

I mentioned my nine zombie apocalypse books earlier, and how I polled my fans to learn that my price was too high for the Genre. Let's rewind briefly, to why I ran that poll in the first place.

I had this 9-book series that was losing money. At 9 books long I should have been making beautiful readthrough and reaching more readers than ever, but I wasn't, so I started looking at my numbers like never before. I looked at sales and readthrough (as we discussed in the Research stage), and realized that readthrough was poor, as low as 3% to book 9.

Sales numbers told me the biggest big drop off in readers came from book 1 to 2. Reviews however were solid across the series, however, except for book 3 which was a little lower, and there were hardly any reviews on the latter books. I had some data, but I needed to know the 'why'. I could only think of one way to find out this 'why' - direct from the horse's mouth. I decided to ask the people who'd been doing the dropping off, my fans.

I put together a newsletter that linked to a simple Google form questionnaire (easy and intuitive to make here www.google.com/forms/about/) - with 3 questions:

- Which book did you drop off on?
- Why?
- How would you fix it so you didn't drop off?

These are simple and clear questions you might want to try yourself, if you're considering polling your fans. Readthrough drop-off is perhaps one of the best things they can tell us about, because while they might not know how to fix a poorly aligned book, or how to make a well-aligned book better, they will certainly know the reason they stopped reading an author whose work they enjoyed at the start.

So I sent these questions out to some 5,000 members on my newsletter, not expecting much. A handful of replies, maybe? I decided to incentivize responses with two $25 Amazon tokens offered in a raffle draw. This was extremely valuable information to me, easily worth far more than $50. To hire an editor to analyze all 9 books, then around 800,000 words, could cost tens of thousands.

Well. As soon as I sent the email, responses started pouring in immediately. I could hardly turn away from the results before another response popped through - many of them with long, thought-out comments as to where and why they dropped off the series. I was amazed. Within 24 hours I had 78 responses.

I had no idea I would get that - or that so many would be so happy to offer their thoughts and expertise. It brought me a surplus of suggestions, and what did they say? Let's take a look.

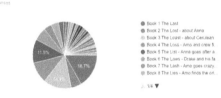

All right, this was some real data. It looked like Books 1, 3, 4 and 5 were the culprits. So, what was it about those books? I asked and they answered. Here's a brief summary of some of their key comments:

- Cost. Many people talked about the price (and number) of books. 9 books at $4.99 each added up to over $40, which was very high compared to other books in the Genre!
- Too complex. Many people talked about how they wanted more of the character from the first book, and less twistiness showing similar events from different perspectives at different times. They wanted the narrative straightened out.
- Non-zombie pseudoscience. While you might think the zombie Genre allows a lot of room for strange science fiction and near-fantasy events to occur, you would be wrong. My readers accepted that zombies could happen, but after that they weren't interested in anything too wacky.
- Brutality. While zombies are a Horror Genre, my

readers said I'd gone too far. Tone it down a bit, keep the hero a wholesome good guy and don't go too dark.

Phew! That was a lot to take on, but I absorbed it in fascination and immediately began thinking about how to fix these Genre-related problems. Over a period of time, here's what I did:

- Cost. I combined all nine books into a single box set, then put that box set up for only 99c. Crazy, but this is what my comparable authors were doing.
- Too complex. This took time, but I essentially restructured and simplified every book in the series, cutting the narrative twistiness right back and straightening everything out neatly. Now the 9 books clock in at around 600,000 words, that's 200,000 words of complexity gone!
- Non-zombie pseudoscience. This required me to cut where I could and simplify where I couldn't.
- Brutality. I reduced the gore and cruelty throughout, returned my hero wholly to the light side and made the read a smoother, nicer experience.

This was obviously a great deal of work. And did it work?

The answer was a resounding, and rapid, yes. Putting the box set up at 99c felt crazy, as I mentioned earlier, but in combination with all the other changes I made, my Kindle Unlimited page reads skyrocketed. People were suddenly reading through and leaving reviews for the entire series.

They were positive! Some were negative, but at least

they'd read all the way to the end. I fed everything back into the Cycle and further aligned. For a good year this series really pulled its weight, and I invested all the income from that into the audiobooks, covers, editing and ads for my thrillers (more on that to come).

The key point is, none of this would have happened if I hadn't polled my Genre readers and listened to what they had to say. Maybe give it a try.

ASK A WRITER'S WORKSHOP ABOUT
YOUR DELIVERY

BODY TEXT PRE- / POST-PUBLICATION $2 IN MY LAST GROUP A
FEW HOURS

MOST AUTHORS WILL BE familiar with writers' workshops, where fellow authors get together to read and constructively critique each other's work. They're ubiquitous in pretty much all cities and towns the world over. I was once a member of one which held marathon sessions for up to 6 hours, as we worked through 10 manuscripts up to 10,000 words in length each (which had to be pre-read for homework), spending some 30 minutes giving comments on each.

To find such a group near you, you need only run an Internet search or try www.Meetup.com, which hosts a very large number of such groups. Most will be free or include a nominal weekly/monthly fee.

These groups can be invaluable for developing line-by-line craft, working on your punctuation, grammar, spelling, crafting snappy beginnings, developing short stories, and so forth. Everything other writers know, they will pass on to you, as you do likewise for them.

I benefited enormously from being a member of such groups. Not only did I make friends with fellow authors and build a support network, I also kept on working on my craft, and workshopped a number of short stories that later went on to sell to pro-paying magazines.

The negatives of a writers' workshop are where it gets more interesting for us, as we seek Genre Mastery. The key negative is that the writers in your group are quite unlikely to have ever thought about the marketing side of the publishing equation. They are less likely to be independent authors and more likely to be seeking traditional publication, where the publishing company will handle their Promise for them, the cover, title, blurb as well as making editorial changes to the Delivery, the body text itself. These writers probably haven't given too much thought to Genre Mastery or about how to reach the reader.

Most likely you'll have some poets in your group, too, some Fantasy authors, some Literary, some Thrillers, but I wager few will really understand or care about the expectations of the readers in their respective Genre. This means it's quite likely that every piece of feedback these writers give you, while well-intentioned and potentially expert in its own way, will be uninformed by the realities of the market.

I have workshopped some incredibly strange things before, including a short story called Trombone Joe, about a character who could play his genitalia as a trombone, thereby moving the world toward peace and harmony, and not once did anyone tell me: "Um, Mike, cool idea, but this will never sell."

They can help you work on your descriptions, your story structure, your craft, but they can't help you move your stories closer to what the audience want, unless of course they have cracked this themselves, and are selling big-time. In which case, grab onto them with both hands and never let go. You've found yourself a mentor.

Another problem with writers' workshops is that they struggle to handle novels. The Delivery. Full novels are where the readers are and where the money is, but I don't know of any writers' workshop that'll sit down and read your whole novel from start to end then get together to discuss it. They may have a system for parsing your novel out into ten bits, but this approach will probably take most of a year to run through, and will look nothing like the average reader's experience of reading your book.

At that level, they can't focus on the overall story. It's hard to feel the flow, the tropes, the motifs as they develop. In any one session, workshoppers are going to focus on what they can help you with, which are the lower level, line-by-line issues of description, grammar, word choice, tone and so on.

So, while I highly recommend them to work on your micro-level craft, I don't think they're the places to work on your macro-level Genre storytelling chops.

START A 99 DESIGNS COVER CONTEST

COVER PRE-/POST-PUBLICATION $300-500 4-5 HOURS ACROSS SEVERAL DAYS

Now we move into the domain of the experts, and for this we're going to have to pay. You knew this stage was coming. To get real expertise, at some point we've got to step out of the barter economy and start parting with cold, hard cash. But I'm not from the school of paying thousands just to publish a book.

Rather, I'm about bootstrapping as much as possible. Get great value, don't trust any one expert so much that their stamp gets imprinted indelibly on your work, and most importantly of all, keep learning. As such, I recommend paying no more than $300-500 for your cover, and that you get it from www.99Designs.com.

You could go cheaper, or even try to self-make your own cover, but you probably shouldn't. Plenty of sites offer incredibly cheap pre-made covers, but they're mostly garbage, and possibly use stock images that are not properly paid for. Plenty of sites charge far more, but the result's going to be about the same in the end. Plenty of people try to design their own cover, but unless you're already a graphic designer/artist, it's going to take you many hours to make something that's not going to compete at a professional level.

What about Asking about an existing cover, though, you may ask? Well, some cover designers have offered cover appraisal services in the past, but they get swamped with demand and cancel. Generally speaking, the only time you're going to get a cover designer's opinion on your cover is when you're paying them to make it for you. And the best way to get that cover is 99 Designs.

The way 99 Designs works slots beautifully into the Genre Mastery Cycle, because it is an extremely iterative process. When you commission a cover through them, you start a contest between multiple cover designers and artists, who will all bid for your project with fully realized covers. You then score each design out of five, which all the designers can see, thereby steering them toward what you like best. You can also give feedback directly, and request as many revisions as you want as long as the process goes on.

The process begins with a 4-day qualifying round, where any designer can submit and resubmit their ideas according to your design remit. You make revisions throughout this period. Another 4 days follow in the qualifying round where you work with the designers you've got and narrow them down to six for the final round. Until day 8, you have a full money-back guarantee. Next you select the top 6 designers for the final round, guaranteeing that you'll pay, and work for another 3 days with these designers to develop your cover. After this you have another 14 days to make up your mind before you have to choose. You can also easily buy more than one cover design, if you want to hedge your bets, for a reduced rate.

I think this is an incredible offer and an incredible process. In my personal experience it has been transformative, as the sheer number of designs you get, combined with the speed of iteration, really spin up the virtuous circle of what you think you want and what you need.

To that end, setting up your cover design guidelines is essential. 99 Designs asks you to suggest color schemes, select the type of book design you're looking for, asks about the book contents, provides a space for you to drop sample images, and offers ample opportunities for you to say what you want.

So what should you say? Well, as much as you can about your Genre, but honestly, not too much. Here we want to lean on the expertise of the range of designers, hoping some of them know more than we do. What I suggest foremost is two things:

- You provide them with a link for one or two of the top 100 bestseller lists for your Genre. Not individual books from those lists, unless you're really confident it's a great match for your book, but rather the whole list. Say something like, 'I want my cover to fit in but also stand out amongst these covers'.
- You can also be a little more specific, and offer a type amongst these covers (e.g., in the Romance Genre, you might want a steamy cover showing man chest, or a pastoral holiday scene, or an illustrated shot of two figures). So, you might say something like, 'OK, I need a Spanish villa in the background, illustrated style, some sea view, and two figures on the balcony. Colors should be blue, yellow and pink, and make the contrast pop (really stand out).'

Once you've given this guidance, you'll start getting dozens of cover ideas thrown at you. Some will be poor, and that's fine. Mark them as 1-star or reject them outright if they're not even close. Some will be strong, mark them with 2 or 3 stars. Other designers will see what you're approving and disapproving and take their lead from you. There'll be some cross-pollination amongst designers. This might be annoying for them, but it's great for us.

This process is how I came up with the current covers for my thriller series, and the cover for this book you're holding in your hands. For this book, I gave the category bestseller lists for self-publishing and book marketing, said I wanted a rocket and Genre symbols in the cloud, and received very many designs.

One was a clear winner from the off, very simple and stark with bold text, which the designer then she adapted to my feedback, until another designer came in with a similar but much better design. I then worked on this cover with him, until I put up a poll of the two covers on my marketing critique group. They approved the second cover by a wide margin, and there we go. A few comments popped up that it looks a little kiddy and may not really demonstrate 'mastery', but that's OK, I like it and so did most of the feedback. It's possible that somewhere further down the Cycle, maybe in a year or two, I'll come up with a better concept for the cover, and maybe I'll change it then.

So, yes. A transformative process. I credit it for producing my current thriller cover, and to some extent my strong sales. In that case I shared the Vigilante Justice and Terrorism thriller category bestseller lists, asked for a dark cover, picked an action-packed scene from the book to depict (a guy with a gun running toward a burning building), and let the designers have at it. As before, I received some fantastic work, worked with multiple designers, watched the cross-pollination happen, ran a poll and here's where I landed:

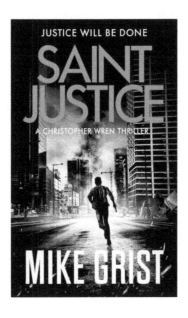

This is the cover currently on the book, and the one that is selling around 100 copies a day. It clearly made a difference. It's dark, has movement, the guy is running somewhere, has great contrast, strong fonts and makes an impact at thumbnail. It shows the reader pretty clearly what's coming in this book. Dark-tinged anti-terror action. I love it, to boot, which is always nice.

So, 99 Designs. Far better, in my view, than hiring any one designer and getting 2 or 3 possible designs max from one person's perspective, with limited revisions. You'll have more designs and revisions than you'll get anywhere else, all for very competitive prices.

There are several tiers of pricing for getting an eBook cover (slightly more expensive if you include the print cover).

I went with Silver for $499 and 60 designs guaranteed both times and was very happy. I don't think you need to spend any more than this.

In short, it's great, and fits perfectly into the virtuous circle we're looking to spin up.

COMMISSION OTHER COVER DESIGNERS

COVER PRE-/POST-PUBLICATION $50-500 3-4 HOURS ACROSS SEVERAL DAYS/WEEKS

WHILE I LOVE the 99 Designs system and will primarily use it going forward, there are very many other cover design experts you can also hire, who will provide you with a solid cover to your specification, and use their Genre knowledge to help you get there. Many of these I've used before. Here are several that I can recommend:

- www.deviantart.com - In my early self-publishing days I used the artist portfolio site Deviant Art a great deal. Deviant Art has forums where you post a paying gig (https://www.deviantart.com/forum/jobs/offers/), and artists reply and share their portfolios.

There's no protection whatsoever, so go in armed with that knowledge, but the prices are incredibly low, and the quality can be fantastic. I got my first 4 early zombie covers done by an artist through Deviant Art, incredibly detailed illustrations that we went back and forth on multiple times, for $100 or less.

Here's that example:

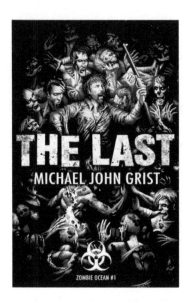

For this cover, I was very early in my Genre Mastery process, and wasn't even looking at zombie books for inspiration. I looked instead at the cover of Andy Weir's The Martian, which showed a guy in a spacesuit getting swallowed up by a red dust storm.

I thought it was a cool concept and asked the artist to reproduce that with zombies. I added the fonts myself. I didn't get any expert opinion, and you won't be surprised to hear I landed nowhere near what the genre looked like. Because it's illustrated, it looks like a comic book. It doesn't have the standard red/brown/fiery colors of a zombie apocalypse book.

It sold OK, but not great. I began to realize at this stage, 2015, that I needed outside help from not just an artist, but a cover design pro who would make me a cover, including fonts, with the genre firmly in mind. So, at this stage, I went to a company.

There are two main cover design companies that I know and would recommend:

- www.Damonza.com - A company created and run by Damon Freeman, which uses a number of cover designers whose work Damon oversees, which will help you get a cover aligned with your genre. Prices are not cheap, currently starting at $645 for an eBook cover, but they do know Genre. When I was getting my zombie books redone, I went to Damonza with a reasonably loose brief - something using photographic manipulation, with a thriller vibe, with ruins and zombies in the background. They produced 3 or 4 draft efforts, we worked together, and this is what we came up with:

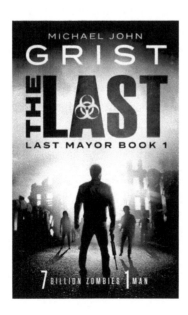

This was a major improvement, and the book immediately began to sell. In color, contrast, setting and font it was way more on target. If I'd gone to Damonza from the start, maybe this is what I would have gotten, but maybe not. It's important to remember, the more restrictions you give to your cover designer, the more they'll try to follow them. The more you trust their judgment, the more they'll roll with their own expertise. It's a balancing act. Do you trust them? Or do you want to inform yourself? Or do you want to try to meet in the middle?

- www.Bookscovered.co.uk - This is another company I've seen produce amazing covers. They produce covers for lots of top indie authors, with a solid portfolio and great credibility. The guy who runs this company, Stuart Bache, has a book on covers and a sub-course available through Mark Dawson's Self-Publishing Formula. Sometimes he'll chip in on the SPF Facebook group with advice and comments on covers provided for critique. He's always worth listening to. His eBook price starts at around $550 dollars.

COMMISSION A BLURB COPYWRITER

BLURB PRE- / POST-PUBLICATION $297 1-2 HOURS ACROSS
SEVERAL DAYS / WEEKS

WRITING YOUR BLURB IS HARD. We all know that. At some stage we've all banged our fingers against the keys (certainly not skimping on the delete key!) until they bleed, then banged away some more. In the Research stage we looked at some techniques to help with this, like overwriting and word clouds, followed up with aligning what you came up with through the earlier Ask stages - but what if that's not working for you?

Sometimes the blurb may prove to be an uncrackable nut. This may be a sign that your body text is too far out of alignment to encapsulate in a snappy blurb. In those cases, I'd recommend you take a look at more closely aligning your body text to Genre - often when the body text aligns, the blurb will fall into place.

But in the event you either don't want to alter the body text, or altering it still doesn't help crack the blurb, it may benefit you to hire an expert set of eyes to craft a blurb on your behalf. They may be able to crack that nut in a way that you can't do yourself. If it comes to that, I'd recommend the following service, as I've seen the work produced on many occasions and can attest it is solid, if expensive:

- www.bestpageforward.net/blurbs - A service set up by Bryan Cohen, a science fiction author with copywriting experience. At first, I believe he wrote all the blurbs himself, now I think he works with a team. The current price for one book is $297, for which you'll receive the blurb as well as Facebook ad copy and ten short pieces of Amazon ad copy. There are discounts if you bulk-order multiple blurbs at once.

Several fellow authors in my marketing critique group have received Bryan Cohen blurbs. One benefit is that these blurbs have both have lifetime refund guarantee, and a rewrite guarantee. If at any time after they provide your blurb, you're not happy with it, they will provide a rewrite for free, or you can ask for your money back.

That's pretty good and allows you peace of mind as you Cycle different blurbs through your sales page (more in stage 3). If the first blurb doesn't work, you simply send it back and ask for another. If none work, get your money back and go back to the drawing board

As a last last resort, you could always look at websites like www.fiverr.com (very cheap) or www.reedsy.com (more expensive) to hire someone who'll write a blurb for you. I can't attest to these services, having never used them myself, but if you're at your wit's end and need help, maybe you'll find in there.

HIRE A BODY TEXT EDITOR

BODY TEXT PRE-/POST-PUBLICATION $1000-2000+ WEEKS TO MONTHS

HIRING an editor for your body text is going to be the largest cost you'll face, and I'm going to caution you to do it as cheaply as possible, extracting as much value as you can from the deal.

You can do this with editors by paying for Manuscript Assessments rather than Developmental Edits, getting Proofreading rather than Line Edits, self-editing to the limit of your expertise, and then getting Beta Reads where necessary to respond nimbly to reader feedback.

Here are the four main types of editing:

- Manuscript Assessment. The editor reads the book and produces a few-page response outlining strengths and weaknesses covering plot, character, setting and maybe Genre alignment, suggesting any changes they think ought to be made. I like a good Manuscript Assessment, but it should be reasonably cheap. I wouldn't pay more than a few hundred dollars for this, $500 max for a full-length novel from a top-tier editor, though I've seen many editors charging thousands. Don't pay thousands for this - get beta readers instead.

- Developmental Edit. Like a Manuscript Assessment, but they'll go deep and they'll either make the big changes for you, or they'll work with you on making them. It'll cost thousands. I don't recommend this, as you're outsourcing too much to someone else's judgment. You'll have no idea if they steered you well or poorly until you put the book on sale and find out if it works. Better to let the readers themselves steer you later on down the Cycle.
- Line Editing. Here the editor is going to leave the big issues alone and focus on your craft at the word, sentence and paragraph level. They'll be rewriting your words, and most likely charging thousands, and potentially changing your intent. I don't recommend this. If your craft is poor, join a writer's workshop and improve it.
- Proofreading. The polishing stage of editing, where they won't make any changes except to correct grammar, spelling, punctuation and maybe continuity errors. You can get this for a hundred dollars or so for a full-length novel, and I wouldn't pay much more.

From that list the only one I recommend is a Manuscript Assessment, and then only if you can get it from a top editor with experience working on chart-topping books in your Genre, for a sub-$500 price.

These are a rare breed. You may not find any. I was lucky enough to find one a few years back via the website www. reedsy.com. Many editors there will charge you $2,000+ for a

Manuscript Assessment, meaning a 5-page report, half of which will probably be the plot summary. That's a hard no.

The one I found charged $350 and laid out a lot of hard truths that I partly took on board and partly deferred, leading to changes in my thriller that definitely helped align it to Genre. Primarily, this editor recommended I remove extra points of view, and stick to the main hero's perspective entirely.

Good stuff. But worth $350? Perhaps. Certainly not worth $2,000, not when you can get the same advice from a dozen different perspectives, far cheaper and faster, from paid beta readers.

CYCLE THROUGH BETA READERS

BODY TEXT PRE-/POST-PUBLICATION $50-100 1-2 WEEKS

I ADORE USING PAID beta readers. These are generally enthusiastic amateurs who love to read, often students at university or retired folks looking to make a little pocket money, who are willing to read your book then provide some kind of 'reader report' much like a manuscript assessment, but for far cheaper than a professional editor, usually between $50-100.

Perhaps the greatest beauty of beta readers is the way they can accelerate the Cycle's virtuous circle. Because there are so many of them, and because they're so affordable, they fall beautifully into an iterative process. Whenever you need to, you get a beta reader, spot a problem, make a change. After that's fixed, you can get a different beta reader, who won't see the old problem because it's gone, but may spot a different problem. You make that change too. The flywheel keeps spinning, and with every update you'll likely notice improvements in your sales, readthrough and reviews.

So, what do these beta readers cover in their reports? Each person is different and has a different offering with a different pricing dependent on word count, but generally you get comments on plot, character, setting, Genre, strengths and weaknesses, suggestions, tropes, that kind of thing. You should always make it clear you're looking for them to tell you what isn't working in your book, rather than just saying nice things as a way to make the client (you) happy.

To achieve this, ask focused questions drawn from any other feedback you've had from across the Cycle. Here's a few examples drawn from my actual experience in making requests of beta readers:

- 'I've had some feedback from readers about the book being baggy in places - though I don't know which places. If you had to cut 10% from this book, which part would you cut and why?'
- 'I've heard from readers that the book is very violent at times (or the plot is confused, or the hero is too indestructible, or whatever the issue is) but I don't know where these standout places are. Can you point out any you come across?'
- 'This book gets good reviews on Amazon, but only 20% of people go on to read book 2. I want to get that number closer to 100% - can you offer any suggestions as to why they're not reading further, and what I might do to improve this?'

The answers you get will almost certainly surprise you. They'll be unknown unknowns straight from the reader experience. Sometimes I hire two beta readers at the same time, to both look at the same version of a given book. Usually, they only take 1-2 weeks to read, so I'll put a pin in any changes I have in mind and wait to get their consensus.

Sometimes they agree. When that happens, there's a pretty good chance they've got a point. Wonderful, especially if it links up with other feedback points from across the Cycle. I have to take that on board and make changes. Other times they'll disagree, or just pick up on different things. That's fine.

It's important to remember that beta readers are generally not experts. What they are is genuine readers, ideally ones who love your Genre. They will give you their honest emotional reaction. What you then do with that is up to your own best judgment.

Now, where can you get your beta readers?

The website www.fiverr.com is all I've needed to use. It's a gigging site where you can hire anyone to do pretty much pretty much anything, priced at anything from $5 and up. Simply go to Fiverr and do a search for Beta Readers to start your journey. Narrow your search term by 'romance novel' or thriller novel' or whatever you like. You can further narrow the results by Top Rated, Level One, Level Two and New Sellers. You can also select only Pro Services. Naturally the higher up the ranking system these beta readers are, the more they'll charge you. New sellers can cost peanuts, sub-$50 at times. The fewer reviews they have, the more you take your chance with them, but since the amounts are so low (and since Fiverr has a robust system for dealing with unsatisfied clients), you could hire 20-30 beta readers in an iterative sequence for a single book, all for less than the price of one modest Developmental edit.

In my eyes, there is no contest here. I've done more than 10 such beta reader reports for my thriller 'Saint Justice'. If any new issues pop up over time, I'll likely get more. I kind of love the process. Wouldn't we all love to be able to hover on the reader's shoulder as they read our work judging their expression as they hit an exciting part, a funny part, a steamy part. Is it working?

Beta readers give us that answer. Give them a try.

ALIGN YOUR PROMISE AND DELIVERY TO GENRE

COVER, TITLE, BLURB, BODY TEXT PRE-/POST-PUBLICATION
$0 CONSTANTLY

AS WITH DEFINING in the Research stage, we should aim to be aligning every time we Ask. One key word to remember is *iteration*. Just like with subsequent generations of iPhones, your book will be getting better with every little bit of feedback you receive, smoothing obstacles standing in the way of the reader's journey.

Smash that obstacle! Knock it into alignment.

Of course, it's up to you how far you go here. The calculus you need to always bear in mind as you're aligning is that old chestnut: Art and Commerce.

Have you written your book primarily for yourself? For you and a few other like minds? For a modestly populated middle ground? For a broad swath of the populace? Or for everyone?

The further you go toward everyone in the mainstream, the more you're going to have to align. How far you want to go toward the Commerce end of the spectrum is entirely up to you, and your level of comfort.

I've faced this challenge with the exact book you currently hold in your hands. I sent a draft copy (in line with the Genre Mastery Cycle) to several trusted beta readers from my marketing critique group in several iterative rounds, and they came back to me with a number of unknown unknowns:

- There was either too much or not enough of me in the book. In the earliest draft, the opening chapter told my story of trials and tribulations in some depth. Some said they'd prefer to get right into the theory and usable data. I didn't want my story to get in the way of the content, so I shifted direct to theory, then in the next round several said they wanted more of my story as an intro. I put a certain amount back in. Now I hope it's a happy medium.
- The tone was a little money-focused, as if the book was only for people interested in becoming millionaires from their writing. This was really an artefact of my frequent shorthand of talking about 'making sales' as a way of saying 'finding more readers and getting my work out into the world'. I didn't want to make authors across the Art/Commerce spectrum feel this book was not for them, however, so I shifted the tone toward 'reaching more readers', however each author defines that.

In this case, aligning to better match the expectations of these readers was a welcome and simple enough step. So I made these changes. I'm making them right now. I will probably continue making them, as I put this newly aligned version of the book (Master Your Genre 2.0, perhaps?) on sale to you, and hope to hear your thoughts on it. This is the Cycle in action.

You'll probably face similar choices with your alignment. The changes for this book were easy and relatively painless, but it won't always be that way. I've found it very hard at times, as I've described with my Thrillers. At some point you'll probably face painful cuts and changes, and you won't be sure you want to make them.

That's fine. One thing I recommend in that case is to open up a version of your book, pre-save it as 'Book Title - alt', and start to play around. You may fear how hard and painful it might be to make the changes, or that it may compromise your vision, but we're just playing here, so put the fear aside. You're in the 'alt' document. The master document is still right there. Nobody can take that away from you.

So give it a try. If you want to, start making some of the changes. You might be surprised by how easily they come, and how little they actually impact your vision. I know this has happened for me. Cutting the dark and violent stuff from my Thrillers actually proved very simple and pain-free, once someone pointed the problem out to me and I'd gotten over the hump of accepting it'd be a good thing to try. Once I'd done it speculatively in the 'alt' document, I was invested in this new version, and found I could no longer justify keeping all that darkness in. If anything, it was getting in the way of my deeper vision.

It might go the same for you. It might not. Maybe give it a try, it probably won't hurt nearly as much as you think, and it just might help.

KEY POINTS

- Ask a Facebook group for advice on your cover, title or blurb.
- Join or create a marketing critique group in person, where you can ask for advice.
- Poll people you know on social media.
- Use Pickfu to poll potentially thousands of people within hours about simple questions or choices.
- Poll your newsletter fans about your Delivery and readthrough using Google forms.
- Join a writer's workshop to work on your craft and tone.
- Start a 99 Designs cover contest to see a great and broad range of ideas for your next cover.
- Hire a cover designer on Deviant Art, Damonza or Books Covered.
- Commission a copywriter to write your blurb.
- Hire a cheap manuscript assessment editor for less than $500, if you can find one.
- Hire a dozen beta readers in iterative sequence for

the same book, and ask them specific questions to expose off-Genre parts of our book.

- Open up an 'alt' document and start using all this feedback to better align your Promise to your Delivery. Decide later if the 'alt' document will become the new master or not.

3

_____

SELL & REFINE

THE FINAL STAGE of the Genre Mastery Cycle, which actually has no real beginning or end but is actually a constantly turning flywheel homing in on a more aligned version of your book, is to take it to your audience.

That's right. Your actual audience. You're going to run your own split test direct to your genuine readers, through the authentic reader journey (go to a shop site, browse for a Promise they like and buy it), by putting the latest version of your book on sale. This is going to tell you everything you need to know about the success of any changes you've made.

At this stage, some may be tempted or feel compelled to take the existing book down from shop sites and upload a whole new listing. I recommend strongly against doing this. For eBooks, while some of the big online shops may suggest you take down the previous version and start up a fresh listing if you make significant changes, there's really no one enforcing this. And why should they?

If you were swapping out your contents completely, as in substituting a highly-ranked Genre fiction book for 500 pages of copy-paste Wikipedia pages, for sure, you shouldn't be making sales and page reads fraudulently off the previous book's reviews.

But we're not doing anything like that. We're iterating the same book and the same story. We're actually making it better aligned to reader expectation. I have changed covers, titles, blurbs and body texts significantly many times and re-uploaded on the same listing and never had a problem.

Now, you may worry readers will get confused, but this is minor risk to run. Regarding, covers, titles and blurbs, traditional publishers frequently alter, update and refresh these on their backlist titles. Regarding changes to the body text, your readers are unlikely to read the same book again, so why should they mind?

I've made changes to later books in my series even as readers were carrying through from the original cut of book 1. Main characters who I'd killed were suddenly now alive. Some names were different. How many complaints have I received? Zero. They either figure it out or maybe they think I made a mistake. It's OK. All will become clear.

However - you will need to take down a paperback book if you change its title, then re-upload a new listing. This is actually a simple and painless experience, at least on Amazon. You unpublish the paperback, de-link it from the eBook, publish the new paperback, then link it to the eBook again.

Easy. All your reviews populate across to the new paperback from the eBook.

If you have audiobooks you can do this too, at least if you're going through Audible/ACX. I've changed the covers, blurbs, titles and even audio tracks of my audiobooks several times. You just email support@acx.com and ask them to do it, and provide all the details they require. If you change the title, you'll have to get your narrator to re-record your opening and closing credits, but that's about 20 seconds of audio, and shouldn't be a problem or costly at all.

So, ultimately, you should always upload your new version right on top of the old one. It's the only way to keep your eBook reviews, and definitely the easiest, best move.

SELL AND ANALYZE VIA A SPLIT TEST

COVER, TITLE, BLURB, BODY TEXT POST-PUBLICATION $0
SEVERAL WEEKS - MONTHS

A SPLIT TEST is when you try out different options and see which one works best. We've done mock split-tests with our cover polls on Facebook and via PickFu in the last section, but the ultimate split test is to simply put the book up for sale on a bookstore and see if it sells. Keep meticulous records. Compare that to sales across another date range.

To make the results as scientific as possible, there are a lot of things to bear in mind when running a test like this, as you obviously can't run them simultaneously. You only have one book, so the test will have to go consecutively. Things to keep in mind:

- You'll want to cover the same period of time, i.e. - Monday to Sunday, whether that's a weeklong or longer. The longer you run the split-test for, the better the data.
- You'll absolutely want to keep all the other three elements of your book the same. One key factor of scientific experimentation is to control your variables, and here we're only varying one at a

time. So if you want to test your cover options, for example, then only vary the cover, don't change your title, blurb or body text at all while you're running the split-test, so as not to muddy the results. Same goes for any of those variables. Pick one (could be the blurb next) and only vary that, while keeping the rest unchanged.

- You'll want to keep any promotion/marketing as consistent and unchanging as possible, as it'll throw your results off. This'll get you to a baseline of sales, where you'll be able to see the effects of your changes more clearly.
- You'll need at least two versions of the element you want to test. This could be your old cover vs. your new cover, your new blurb vs. your old blurb, etc.
- You'll want to run a consistent budget of ads (I recommend Facebook ads) to drive some traffic to the book.

Of course, you don't have to run Facebook ads. However, if your book is currently invisible in the bookstores, changing one element will make no difference. Running Facebook ads gives us access to the coldest, most-targeted audience possible. If they click your ad, then get to your page, and read your blurb, and maybe click your Look Inside to see the body text, then buy the book? Yup, the new element has done the job.

So, Facebook ads.

USE FACEBOOK ADS FOR TESTING

COVER, TITLE, BLURB POST-PUBLICATION $5+/DAY FOR ADS
1-2 HOURS TO SET UP

ON FACEBOOK you can target by age, gender, geographical area, interest and various other factors. You can make an ad with an image, text, headline and description. I would prepare two simple ads, each one with a different variant of the element you're experimenting with. If it was covers, then you'll want your two alternate book covers in the simplest form possible. Just as with the sales page, you'll want every other element else across these ads to be exactly the same. Targeted to the same audience, with the same text, headline and description.

You'll want to run these ads consecutively, not simultaneously, just as you run the book on the bookstore page consecutively. Sync them up as best you can. Spend whatever budget you're willing to on this split-test experiment. Maybe $5 a day, maybe more. A higher budget will get you faster results. Whatever you spend, it should be exactly the same across the two parts of the test.

So, with a fixed budget, and fixed title, blurb and body text across the bookstore sales page and the ads, and a baseline of sales prior to running these ads and making these cover changes, you'll be in a strong position to see the results of this one-variable experiment. The job after this is to record the sales above the baseline.

If cover A sells more books, cover A may be the winner. If cover B sells more books, B may be the winner. If neither break even, then you'll need to think about your other elements, or readthrough to your other books to see if they're genuinely profitable. If they sell the same, maybe the covers are about equal in quality and in signaling Genre, and you can go with either.

An alternate way to test a large number combinations of covers, titles, taglines and blurbs is through running a Facebook dynamic ad, which will allow you to enter between 5 and 10 different versions of each element then allow the Facebook algorithm to determine which one best suits your target audience and earns the cheapest clicks. Considering this technique more deeply, however, is the province of another book.

MONITOR YOUR SALES CONVERSION, READTHROUGH AND REVIEWS

SALES DATA POST-PUBLICATION $0 WEEKS-MONTHS

THE FOLLOWING analytical tools may be a little advanced, and you may feel your eyes glazing over when we get to the formulas (formulas! You mean mathematical formulas!?) that accompany them, so I want to set your mind at ease as much as I can.

You don't have to do these analyses. If your books are selling well enough that you're breaking even, you may not want to be concerned with them at all. But if your books are not breaking even, and you don't know which part of the Cycle is responsible - is it your Genre targeting, the alignment of your Promise, or the Delivery itself? - then they can be enormously helpful.

First we'll outline what they are, and then we'll talk about how to use the data they provide to diagnose problems with your book's Genre, Promise and Delivery.

Take a deep breath. Here we go.

There are three key analytical tools you can use to know if you've hit alignment and produced a story that your readers love and want more of. They've all been mentioned already in one form or another, but here we'll go a little deeper:

- Sales Conversion
- Readthrough
- Reviews

Sales Conversion

'Conversion' is a real buzzword-sounding marketing term, but I promise it's not as daunting as it seems, and can be extremely useful for checking the power of your Promise (the cover, title and blurb).

Essentially, 'Conversion' is a number that tells us how many people that see your book go on to buy your book. They are 'converted' to, what, the Dark side? Ha ha ha. To your side. So if a hundred people see your book's sales Page, perhaps sent there from your Facebook ads, and all one hundred of those buy the book, that's a 100% conversion rate.

This would be amazing. Your Genre and your Promise (and your ads - which are an extension of your Promise) are beautifully aligned, and the readers love it.

More likely you'll see numbers like 3 books bought out of 100 clicks, which would be a 3% conversion, or 1 in approximately 30.

Here's how Conversion is calculated:

$$\text{Conversion} = \frac{\text{Number of books sold (3)}}{\text{Number of readers sent (100)}} \times 100 = 3\%$$

This is a decent conversion rate. Your Promise is aligned to Genre and doing its job. There are additional variables involved if we're looking at profitability, such as your book's price, how much you're paying for the readers you send from your ads, and how you're targeting your clicks (all matter for a book more focused on advertising), but the Conversion % gives us a great starting point.

Anything better than 3% is looking very good. Anything worse suggests there may be a problem with your Promise, so that's an area you'll want to focus your energy on - more closely defining your Genre and figuring out how to better align your Promise. We'll troubleshoot some common problems shortly.

Readthrough

We encountered this number a couple of times already – it often comes as a percentage, and tell us how many people people read through to another book from you after reading their first. We want as high a number as possible, here, because that means your books are effectively Delivering on their Promise.

You're giving the readers what they want and delighting them on the way. They're going onto the next book by you, which means they're well on their way to becoming fans. High readthrough is also going to really help your bottom line. These days it can cost a lot of money to promote books and convert a browser to a reader. Maybe it will cost more per person to convert them than you earn from selling them the book.,

This would put you in the red. If you pay $3 to convert someone from Facebook to buy your first book, but you only earn say $2 from that book, you're promotion is unsustainable.

Here's where strong readthrough is a lifesaver. If you have 100% readthrough (an amazing figure, pretty unlikely) then each reader will buy another book. It still costs us $3 to convert them to read book 1, but now they're going to read book 2 as well. If book 2 earns us $2 also, suddenly we're making $4! It cost us $3 to convert them, we're making $4, suddenly we're in profit!

The advertising can continue. Even expand!

Readthrough is amazing like this. It's the reason authors often advise to 'write in a series' or 'don't promote book 1 until you have three books out'. They're saying this because promoting a single book is very hard to profit off. But with strong readthrough, you can break even and even make money more easily off a handful of books.

So, how to calculate readthrough?

It's easiest to work out for books in a series, so that's where we'll start. First you want to pick a fairly long time period, say six-months, then you're going to look at the total number of sales you've made for each book in your series. If you sell 100 copies of book 1 and 100 copies of book 2, that would be a 100% readthrough.

As we said, this would be incredible. You instantly know that everyone who buys book 1 is so happy with your Delivery that they went on to buy the next. There's no problem here, and no need to further align your body text.

More likely you'll see numbers like 50 sales of book 2 for 100 of book 1, which would be a 50% readthrough. Here's the formula:

$$\text{Readthrough in a series} = \frac{\text{Sales of book 2 in a given period (50)}}{\text{Sales of book 1 in a given period (100)}} \times 100 = 50\%$$

This is a pretty good readthrough rate. It says your Delivery is reasonably aligned to your Promise and partly doing its job. Anything higher than 50% is looking very good. Anything worse suggests there may be a problem with your Delivery, so that's an area you'll want to focus your energy on - more closely aligning the body text to both your Promise and your Genre.

As you move through a series, you can keep on making this calculation. You could check your readthrough from book 1 to book 3, for example, by substituting your book 3 sales numbers for book 2 in the formula above. Or, if you'd like to know how many people are reading through from book 2 to book 3, then you swap both numbers, book 3 on top, book 2 on the bottom, and calculate. You'll see how many are dropping off after book 2. Hopefully this number will be higher than your book 1 to book 2 readthrough. We're starting to home in our fans.

You can run a similar calculation for books that are not in a series, but it only works if you have one clear 'gateway' book to your writing, as in only one book you're advertising to bring readers in. You simply substitute that gateway book's numbers for book 1 in the calculation above, and swap in any other book in your backlist for book 2.

Reviews

After all that math, reviews are easy. We already talked about reading your reviews, how important it is, and also some ways to take the sting out of bad 1-star reviews.

What you'll want to be looking for is your review rating going up over time. Most shop sites give a star rating out of 5, and you'll want to be as close to 5 as you can get, off as many reviews as possible. Readers look at these ratings. On Amazon, if you can get your rating up to 4.3, it ticks over the magic line that makes the star images round up to four and a half.

When this happens, it's a beautiful day. For most browsing readers, your book just got a high seal of approval.

Four stars is good. Four and a half stars means it's a known quantity.

We're also going to be reading the content of the reviews, to see any refinements we can make. Maybe you fixed some of the alignment problems in the Ask stage, but some of them you ignored, or some you only half-fixed. Readers are going to let you know about it here. Take what they say on board and refine where you agree.

Understanding the Results

To recap these three tools, Sales Conversion is the percentage of people sent from ads that you convert into readers. Readthrough is the percentage of people who bought book 1 and went on to read your later books. Reviews could come on Amazon, Goodreads, private blogs or any other shop site.

Results for these will come in both slow and fast. For Conversion, you should see a difference immediately, as long as you're sending people to your sales page via some kind of ads. Obviously, we want to 'convert' a larger proportion of these clicks to sales.

For readthrough, this could take days or weeks to shift. When I put up the new version of Saint Justice, my first thriller, the sequel started selling more almost right away. If you get that, it's a great sign. People are reading fast. As ever, we're aiming for the highest readthrough possible. 100% would be amazing. Anything above 50% is great in my book. I'm always hopeful to hit at least 70%, and that's an ongoing work in progress.

Reviews will come slowest of all. On a short timeline it may even be hard for you to know which version of your book they bought, and therefore which version they're reviewing. I put up the new version of Saint Justice four months ago now, and am still getting negative reviews for the version before that. Nobody's fault, just the way it is.

Sometimes new reviews will be obvious, because they mention something that's only in the new version. Here, obviously, we want higher star ratings and glowing comments, but fresh negatives will always be useful and help us define, align and refine faster, as long as we don't let the 1-stars go to our hearts. If that happens, take a warm bath in your 5-star reviews to recover.

Remember, 2-star, 3-star and 4-star reviews are likely the thoughts of your genuine readers, who were hunting for your Genre, found your Promise appealing, paid money, read your book, and now are telling you what they think of your Delivery.

Where you can bear it, listen.

REFINE YOUR GENRE, PROMISE AND DELIVERY

COVER, TITLE, BLURB, BODY TEXT POST-PUBLICATION $0
CONSTANTLY

Thus, we come to the last stage of the Genre Mastery Cycle. You've researched to define your book's Genre, asked all kinds of people to help align it to your Promise and Delivery, then road-tested those changes to the target reader by Selling it.

Now the reader speaks, and it's time to refine. Maybe you disagree with them, which is OK. Sometimes there's a Rubicon you won't want to cross, changes you aren't willing to make. You hold fast to your vision and be satisfied with the level of readers you're reaching and sales you're getting.

Alternately, maybe you're just getting going. This first round of feedback could be really building up some steam, with revelations flying thick and fast. It might be time to plunge back into the Cycle with some detailed questions for beta readers, fire up some new word cloud research into comparable blurbs, post some polls for a new cover or a sparkling new tagline.

The Cycle turns, and you'll refine as you wish. You'll definitely know more about your Genre, Promise and Delivery by now. Even if you choose to make no further refinements, your next book will be better aligned to Genre as a result of the work you've done so far, if alignment's what you want. You can reach more readers. Sales can rise. Lives can change. Jump back into the Cycle and give it a spin!

Let's look at some common problems, troubleshoot and diagnose them, and talk about some possible ways to start refining.

Low Conversion, Low Readthrough, Poor Reviews

This is really the trifecta. You can't sell, you don't get readthrough, and your reviews are bad. I'm sorry. Your Promise doesn't align to your Genre, your Delivery doesn't align to your Promise, and your readers emerge neither satisfied or delighted.

It happens.

What should you do? You're going to have to Define, Align and Refine from scratch.

Diagnosis: Genre, Promise and Delivery not aligned.

Treatment options:

- Read your reviews. Even the painful ones. The readers will be telling you something and you need to listen.
- Read widely in the Genre. You need a better grounding in what the Genre expectations are, so you can start to grapple with some of the unknown unknowns you're not seeing. You're off-Genre, but you don't know how. This is like being wildly drunk in the bowling alley. You can't see the lanes.
- Hire a beta reader and ask them why people aren't liking your book. Make it clear you want the

negatives here, not the positives. We want to turn this thing around.

From the above first steps, you should start hitting on some real revelations that'll get the Cycle spinning up. Take it from there, iterate as best you can, go through some more beta reader edits, wait for reviews, work on your blurb, body text, cover as appropriate, and see where it takes you. Good luck!

Low Conversion, High Readthrough, Good Reviews

This is an interesting one - the high readthrough tells us people like your book, once they've read the body text, and the reviews just confirm this. It looks like the problem is with your Promise. It's not aligning to Genre correctly.

This is probably because you're signaling your Genre poorly through the Promise. The few readers who do click through and read it, in spite of your confusing Promise, end up realizing it is their kind of thing. Maybe you need to Define your Genre more, or maybe you just need to Align your Promise more effectively.

Diagnosis: Promise not aligned to Genre.

Treatment options:

- Closely read your reader reviews for hints as to what Genre they think it is. If they ever compare you to other authors or books they read, listen.
- Consider polling your fans. Ask them what subGenre they think your book is in. Maybe offer Genres in a poll, along with prime example books from those subGenres, and ask them to vote which your book is closest to.

- Once you have an idea of your true subGenre, read widely in that Genre, trying to see if your book is a good match. Make a decision about how to define your target Genre.
- After this you're into making a new Promise that is better-aligned. A change to your cover and blurb here could flip everything overnight.

High Conversion, Low Readthrough, Poor Reviews

This is the other side of the problem above - high Conversion tells us your Promise is closely aligned to a Genre, but the low Readthrough suggests you're not actually Delivering that Genre in your body text. It could be that you're off-Genre, it could be craft issues, it could be a lack of urgency propelling the reader to the next book (maybe consider a tiny cliffhanger?)

Diagnosis: Delivery not aligned to Promise.

Treatment options:

- Read your reviews. Somebody will definitely tell you where the mismatch of Genre is. They'll say something like, "I thought this was going to be a Cozy Romance but in the end it was a Zombie Apocalypse saga. What gives?" If multiple reviewers are saying the same thing, you've got your answer.
- With that information, you'll want to read widely in both Genres, the one your Promise is targeting and the one your body text is Delivering. Think hard about which direction you want to go in. In one case, you'll only need to change your Promise to align to the existing Delivery, which is easy

enough, though a cover can be expensive. In the other case, you'll have to change your body text to match the existing Promise. This may be harder. In the worst outcome, you'll have to change both Promise and Delivery to align to some middle Genre you hadn't considered, but which is the best actual match.

- After this, proceed to Sell and Refine to see how our readers like it. Maybe they'll be whole new readers. You may need to jump back into the Cycle to Refine the new package you've got. That's good you're making progress!

Low Conversion, Low Readthrough, High Reviews

This is a strange one, but also one I have experience of - it's where my Cyberpunk trilogy currently lives (which we'll discuss shortly in the Case Study). One possibility to explain this is that you're getting the positive reviews from friends and family. They can inflate your star rating, as long as few other people buy the book.

That's not what's happened in the case of my Cyberpunk books, and it may not have happened to you either. The alternative explanation is you've written something both intense and off- or cross-Genre. It's an experience people value and admire, but not one it's easy to pull them into, and not one they're keen to repeat.

To exemplify this, imagine the Fast and Furious Action movies. Mainstream viewers love them, and could probably binge watch several of them happily in a row. Then consider Schindler's List. After you watch that, would you want to watch another movie on the same topic right away?

Probably not. Schindler's List is intense, fulfilling,

perhaps overwhelming. You're going to need a break. If this is what you were going for with your book, then well done. It was an emotional gut punch. You said something important and really impacted the reader. Getting enough readthrough and reaching enough readers to get the book above the breakeven point may be a big challenge, however.

Diagnosis: Delivery is overwhelming or off-Genre.

Treatment options:

You can try all the usual Cycle options here, reading widely, getting beta readers, aligning and refining, but in the end a book with this profile will be difficult to sell. If you self-published it, you may wish to consider seeking traditional publication. Big publishers have powers to promote intense, cross- and off-Genre works that are not easily available to independent publishers, such as getting influencers to push it, putting it forward for awards and such.

It is a little unlikely that a publisher will want this work if it has already been self-published with a poor sales record, but they may well want your next. Alternatively, you could set out with your next book to write something a little more on-Genre, which is exactly what I did.

I wrote my Zombie books, then I wrote my Thrillers, and at no stage did I feel like I sold out. I went to meet the reader, but I was well within that joyous place where what I wanted to write overlapped with what the reader wanted to read. If you too can find that overlapping space, then listen to your readers to stay within it as the Genre lines constantly ebb and flow, then you'll give your stories the best boost possible to find the kind of readers who'll love and champion them.

Good luck!

KEY POINTS

- Split-test sales of your book, varying only one element of cover, title, blurb or body text at any one time.
- Use Facebook ads to speed up your testing, but continue varying only one element at a time.
- Watch your conversion, readthrough and reviews like a hawk, looking for an upturn and further chances to refine.
- Conversion % measures how many people shift from browsing readers to sales. Anything higher than 3% is pretty good.
- Readthrough % measures how many readers move onto your next book after buying their first. Anything higher than 50% is pretty good.
- Reviews come out of 5-stars, and anything higher than 4.0 is pretty good, with 4.5 being great.
- When your Genre, Promise or Delivery are out of alignment, there are many ways to fix it through the Cycle. In some scenarios, however, it may be

best to learn what you can and move on to writing the next book.

III. Q & A

There may be several questions jostling in the back of your head while you've worked through all these techniques. Let's take a look at them now.

Isn't this selling out?

I totally get this argument and this fear. I've been there. My thrillers in their earliest versions were a strong reflection of how I was feeling at the time I wrote them. They came out dark, violent and quite didactic. I had some points to make, about equality, mental health, human psychology, and by Jove I was going to make them, reader be damned!

But it didn't work. Nobody wants to be lectured. Likewise, readers in my target Genre didn't want to be bludgeoned with violence and darkness either. It's not the Genre they were looking for.

This is why I talk about going to the reader. We all have a point to make or issues we want to raise, or even just the full blast of our creativity to share, but the best way to get readers on board with that is subtly and in small doses.

So be didactic. Be creative. Mash-up Genres. But do it in little bites, leavened out across your entire output.

Is that selling out? OK then. Sign me up. I want to reach readers where they are, not force them to come to me. They want certain things from a Genre. Give that to them, along with a little bit of whatever fresh flavor you're hawking, and they'll love it.

Ultimately, it's your choice. If anyone calls you a sellout, who really cares? Maybe they'll be staying pure to their artistic integrity, far from the bestseller charts, lecturing or bludgeoning a select few, while you'll be getting your creativity & message across subtly and enjoyably to the masses, and making a living while you do it.

Isn't it somehow 'wrong' to keep rewriting a book?

I can kind of understand where this one comes from. In the traditional publishing model rewriting a book may be anathema. When your business model is massive print runs, you've got one shot to get each book right. Screw up with your Genre, Promise or Delivery and that screw up likely lives on forever. Making authorial changes late in the game means adding some kind of correction slip to every printed book, but you couldn't do that more than once per book, or loose-leaf papers would be tumbling out like confetti.

But as indie authors selling primarily via online and Print-On-Demand, we don't face this issue.

We can iterate like Apple producing updated versions of its iPhones. Our books can move from in the red to in the black, from turning readers off to delighting them, within a matter of hours. We can go around and around the Genre Mastery Cycle as many times as we like for any one book, constantly bringing it to greater alignment.

There's nothing wrong with this.

A book doesn't have to be a dead letter. It can be a living thing, ever evolving and improving. Don't believe me? Walt Whitman rewrote his major work of poetry, 'Leaves of Grass', countless times from its first publication in 1855 until his death in 1892. That's 37 years of iterating! Mary Shelley rewrote Frankenstein substantially, and the version we know today is the version she rewrote thirteen years after its first publication. Stephen King rewrote and expanded The Stand twelve years after it was first published. Tolkien rewrote The Hobbit years later. If it's good enough for Walt, Mary, Stephen and J.R.R., it's good enough for me.

Look at your books this way, with the door always open to improvement, and you'll learn exponentially more. You'll write better going forward. You'll sell more. Readers will suddenly start noticing you, because you're going over to where they are, telling stories they want to hear, because you know exactly what they want, because they told you and you listened.

Are you suggesting I get hung up on endlessly editing one book?

I understand this fear and want to be very clear - I am absolutely not advocating getting forever hung up on your first book, or any book. Not at all. I'm talking about achieving the best alignment you can on any one day, making changes, re-uploading your book for sale, then waiting for more feedback to come in while you work on the next.

Improve your backlist while writing better frontlist.

Some authors say never look back at all. I say, why not?

But, as I say, I do totally understand this fear. I have

100% been there, and in those days the advice to never look back, only keep moving forward was essential.

It happened with my epic fantasy book, back before independent publishing was a thing. The only way to get the book out there was through traditional publishing, but the publishers were all saying no, and not one of them gave me a reason why. So I was left to make changes to try and cater to what they wanted, all along with no idea of what they actually wanted, or if any of what I was doing was making any difference.

This was obviously horrible. It took the advice of author guru Dean Wesley Smith espousing 'Heinlein's Rules' to get me through it - in particular rule 3:

You must refrain from rewriting, except to editorial order.

A great rule. I didn't have any meaningful feedback from the gatekeepers that mattered, the agents and the publishers, so I was left to blindly make changes. It was endless and quite hopeless feeling. Then on hearing this rule, I gradually took it on board, and was able to move on.

Then came the renaissance in self-publishing, and everything changed. With the ability to self-publish, the role of gatekeeper moved from the black box of traditional publishing to the open arms of the reading public. If they don't like it, they vote with their dollars. They leave reviews. Consider their reviews your editorial orders. More broadly, consider the Genre Mastery Cycle your editorial guide.

I published my epic fantasies. I published my cyberpunk books. I didn't spend years noodling over them (at least not to the exclusion of all else), and neither will you. When feedback came in, I adapted as best I could, then moved on. Write and edit to the best standard you're capable of on that given day, on the best feedback you can get, then follow Heinlein's 4th and 5th rule:

You must put the work on the market.
   You must keep the work on the market until it is sold.

Exactly this. Put the work up until fresh editorial orders come in from the new gatekeepers, the readers, and then iterate to your heart's content, as you see fit, with changes that can go out the same day you make them. Get the flywheel spinning.

Isn't it better just to write the next book? Lots of authors advise this.

This one's connected to the previous problem, but I want to tackle it head-on, because I think it can be poisonous advice from authors who may not know what they're saying. And I see this one all the time on the various online groups.

First up, absolutely, one of the best ways to sell more books, backlist included, is to sell more frontlist. Lee Child, author of Jack Reacher, said words to this effect in the authormentary 'Reacher Said Nothing', suggesting his prodigious Reacher backlist would dry up if he stopped producing a new Reacher book every year.

Yes, for sure. But Reacher book 1 sold from the off. It had great readthrough from the off. Lee Child mastered his Genre from the off. So for him, definitely, writing more will help. And likewise, if we've mastered our Genre, but we're struggling to make a profit off one or two books in series, more books can almost certainly dig us out. Advertising is so competitive now that we need to sell multiple books to each reader to pay off the sunk ad costs.

In all those cases, for sure, write more books.

But if you haven't mastered your Genre yet, writing more books that also won't align or delight readers is probably a waste of time. We're not in this to get lucky, after all. If you don't understand why your backlist isn't selling, you're totally rolling the dice when you write new books. Maybe they'll hit?

Whether they do or they don't, you won't know why.

Mastery's about knowing why. Listening. Learning. By going through the Genre Mastery Cycle, you'll be doing more than just learning the craft of story, you'll be learning how to tell the stories people want. Writing squarely on Genre is like being good at tenpin bowling. You're bounded either side by the gutters of off-Genre. You can bowl any way you like, curve balls, rockets down the middle, toss a bouncer, but the only way to hit a strike is by staying out of the gutter. And you can't stay out of the gutter if you don't know where it is or respect the fact that it exists.

This is overwhelming. How can I do all of this stuff?

Like we said at the beginning, you don't have to do it all. I've provided all the techniques I used to get to where I am, but you could pick a handful of them, or even just one that you haven't tried before, and get some useful feedback to start your virtuous circle spinning. The biggest step is the first step you take toward the reader.

Once you take one step, you may start to wonder why you

didn't take it sooner. It doesn't hurt anything like you think it will, and that could easily be more than made up for when you see your sales and readthrough increase. If you take just one step closer to the reader, you may well find it a little addictive, and start trying out some of the other techniques to speed the Cycle up. Maybe you'll come up with some new techniques for harvesting feedback! If you do, please share them with me too.

Won't listening to readers stifle my creativity & crush my will to write?

I get this one too. I have felt this too. As I took onboard critique after critique of my thrillers, it went to my heart. It hurt. Making cuts to my thrillers hurt at first, though the sting went away fast as the sales came in. I'm also a slower writer now, because I'm consciously putting gutters either side to block off bad habits I now know I have.

My view is, it's good to put those gutters in. They force me to bowl better. Writing is still fun and fulfilling, but it is harder. Again, this is one of those cases where you need to decide for yourself what you want.

Only fun times as you write, freewheeling on any subject in any order that your muse dictates? Or constantly challenging yourself, trying to squeeze your creative ideas between the gutters of Genre expectation?

It's hard, sure, but I'd say more fulfilling when you manage it. When readers read it and love it. Writing should be play, for sure, but if you want to reach a larger number of readers, get paid or even make this your living, it's also work.

Let's get to work.

What if I spend all this time and effort Cycling my book, and I can't reach any more readers?

I think this is unlikely, but it is possible. I've been through the Genre Mastery Cycle many times for many books, and while it's a powerful tool that can lead to mainstream success, sometimes a book simply cannot be saved. In my experience, this occurs when the book combines disparate Genres in ways that cannot be untangled.

If this happens to you, you won't be alone. I've been there. Sometimes problems with aligning your Genre, Promise and Delivery can be fixed easily. Some with modest effort. Sometimes, however, the problems with Genre alignment may be baked too deeply into the body text to merit changing. In some cases, it would be too difficult, laborious, time-intensive or indeed painful to the author's vision to make the changes necessary to hit a target Genre.

That's OK. Knowing when the Genre Mastery Cycle is useful or not is a skill set all of its own, one you'll develop as you work through the Cycle and your books. Next up is a a case study drawn from my own backlist, exemplifying a lower level of Genre Mastery success, as a way to help calibrate your sense of when to keep working and when to just leave a book well enough alone.

Key Points

- Mastering your Genre is not selling out, it's taking however many steps you're comfortable with to satisfy the reader's expectations while also delighting them with something new.

- It's not wrong to rewrite a book. Many legendary authors have done it before.
- The Genre Mastery Cycle won't is not about endlessly rewriting a book. It's about working rewrites where fresh feedback comes in, that you believe is worth listening to and acting upon. You can do this while writing the next book.
- But - simply writing the next book without understanding why the previous one didn't reach readers like you'd hoped is a recipe for history repeating itself. You have to learn why.
- There's a lot in the Genre Mastery Cycle. Absorb a little at a time, and use whatever seems useful to you.
- Listening to readers can make writing a little harder, as you consider their wants alongside their own. I don't think that's a bad thing. Maybe it ups the challenge. Writing is still fun, within the gutters of your bowling lane.
- Not every book can achieve a wider readership. Learn from these cases and move forward with your head held high.

IV. CASE STUDY

A SCIENCE FICTION TRILOGY

I MENTIONED EARLY in the book that I'd written a trilogy of science fiction books that struggled to find readers - the Ruins Sonata. These were experimental stories with interweaving narratives, set in a far-future post-apocalypse where a psychic vampire character is trying to get our hero, a man who can dive into people's minds, to pull off one last 'mind-heist' and unlock an incredible source of power.

Yes, it's pretty out there.

I wrote this series in 2014/15 and didn't pay much attention to Genre or sales until all three books were out, when I realized I was losing money to promote them.

That was a downer, and took me by surprise. If I couldn't at least break even, I couldn't justify keeping on promoting the books, which meant they would just sink into invisibility on the world's digital bookstores. I didn't want that, so my journey toward the Genre Mastery Cycle began.

In those early days, though, I didn't know much about Genre or how to analyze my sales and calculate readthrough. Only years later did I check readthrough to see it was very low, around 5% to book 2 and less than 1% to book 3. Those are obviously very poor numbers.

Something had to be done. I didn't know what, had no idea really, but I figured it had to be linked to the covers. So over the following five years, I had five different covers made for each book in the trilogy. Let's see how that process fared.

These first three illustrated covers were based on mild Research of other books, but not really focused on science fiction, and with little eye to a specific subGenre, largely because I hadn't been able to define my Genre. The books are hard science fiction in one way, cyberpunk in another, space marine in yet one more, as well as having lots of challenging Literary elements, like interweaving narratives that played with time and perception, along with lots of difficult concepts and invented vocabulary.

As inspiration for these covers, I drew on a Literary book I'd read that had similarly overlapping narratives and a cool-looking maze on the cover. I thought I could go one better, with a maze in a brain, a heart, etc....

In the year that followed, author feedback from the Ask stage (before the current crop of Facebook groups existed and everyone go their news off of a privately owned site called K-boards) told me the cover for book one looked like maggots squirming atop an eyeball. They didn't look like science fiction books, certainly not cyberpunk or those other Genre. I decided I had to get the covers remade.

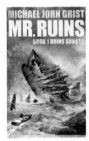  

This second batch were based off some adventure Genre covers that were popular at the time, with big structures dwarfing small figures in the foreground. I was looking to Genre more now, but not really the right Genre, and I didn't know how to get it executed in the right way. These covers depict scenes from various important ruins in the books, and they're beautiful, but they're a strange, flat, old-looking style, so they don't look much like science fiction. These covers did not help the books to sell, so a year or so later I went in for another round.

This time I decided to lean into the 'psychic vampire' side of these stories, and looked to some top-selling covers that featured characters foremost, with the tops of their heads cut off. In those cases, they were photographs, but I decided to go illustrated because I liked that style better personally. However, while these covers were based on Genre research, the popular covers I was mimicking were from the Paranormal Romance Genre, books like Twilight, which my books were very far from. Perhaps I was getting closer, but these covers didn't appreciably help.

At this point I was considering letting the books lie. Maybe there was a way to sell them, an audience of readers out there waiting for them, but I didn't know how to find them. Yet I wasn't quite ready to give up, so I went back for another round.

For these, I was far less specific in my remit to the artist, asking for a science fiction-feeling thriller cover, and that's what I got. It is the closest yet to the right Genre. Maybe with all that red, though, the first book looks like Zombie Post-Apocalypse, which would be misaligned. It did not help with sales, and I did not bother to get books 2 and 3 made individually.

By this time, though, I was starting to get into the Cycle. My zombie books were having success, which gave me confidence these books could do the same. I went in for a more total revamp of not only the covers, but also the titles, blurbs and body texts. Here's what I came up with:

Now, these look like the right kind of Genre, which is Cyberpunk science fiction, with the neon colors. They have new titles after I'd received feedback that the original titles didn't sound like science fiction. They have wholly re-arranged body texts too, with the confusing narrative structure ironed out and the complex concepts better explained - I even wrote a glossary for the difficult terms that remained!

All told, this process has taken years. And the effect?

It's been small. Book 1 sells a little, though I still can't promote it without losing money. Readthrough to books 2 and 3 remains low. I'm glad a few people pick it up and read it, but I've largely come to the conclusion that the body text is too irredeemably off-Genre to ever reach a wide readership. To rewrite the series on-Genre would mean writing almost a completely new trilogy, and I'm not going to do that.

And that's OK. Maybe in the future I'll think of some more comfortable way to align the trilogy to a given Genre and get it into more readers' hands, but I'm not there yet.

This happens. I learned so much through the process, and carried that learning forward to all the books that followed, both my zombie apocalypse series and my thrillers, and to the book you're holding in your hands right now. So if you find your backlist is irredeemably off-Genre, don't despair. We're always learning. Every revelation takes us forward. To quote Winston Churchill:

"Success is not final, failure is not fatal; it is the courage to continue that counts."

Key Points

- Even with all the best intentions in the world, and a willingness to align quite far, some books can't reach a wider readership.
- Learn from that. Pick yourself up. Dust yourself down. Go on to the next.

V. MORE WAYS INTO THE CYCLE

A USEFUL WAY of getting into the Genre Mastery Cycle may be to start with the fastest and cheapest techniques, as these require the least effort on your part for maximum bang. Another way may be to focus primarily on one element of the Promise or Delivery at a time, and a third may be to focus on what you can do pre-publication - this may be especially useful if you're looking to submit to agents or traditional publishers.

To that end, here the techniques are again, laid out first in order of both cost and time, secondly organized by element, and thirdly organized by those you can do pre-publication.

By Time and Cost

$0

Less than 30 mins:

- Study top 100 comparable covers
- Be inspired by comparable titles
- Check comparable prices, formats & KU status

- Read your Reviews
- Word cloud analysis of top 100 blurbs
- Overwrite top 100 blurbs
- Ask a Facebook group about your Promise
- Poll people you know on your Promise

30 mins - 2 hours

- Write the blurb first
- Use movie classification to define tone

Weeks - months

- Sell and analyze via a split test
- Monitor your Conversion, Readthrough and Reviews
- Define your Genre
- Align your Promise and Delivery to Genre
- Refine your Genre, Promise and Delivery

$1 - $100
30 mins - 2 hours:

- Outsource cover research to K-lytics
- Outsource title research to K-lytics
- Ask a marketing critique group about your Promise
- Poll the masses on your Promise via Pickfu
- Poll your fans on your Delivery
- Ask a writer's workshop about your Delivery
- Use Facebook ads for testing

1-2 weeks

- Cycle through beta readers

$100 - $500
Several days-weeks:

- Start a 99 Designs cover contest
- Commission other cover designers
- Commission a blurb copywriter

$1000 - $2000+
Several weeks - months:

- Hire a body text editor

$1000 budget

Thus far I've aimed to avoid being prescriptive with the techniques in this book - you can discover them and use them in any order, in any way that feels best to you. But what if I was giving advice to myself? If I was starting out with a $1000 budget, no books as yet published but maybe one in the tank, what would I spend my time and money on?

Here's what I might say.

First up, so much depends on where you're at in your writing career. Do you have a strong level of craft that readers respond to? Are you a great storyteller that people want to listen to? The techniques in this book can help you bend those things to be better aligned to the reader, but they're not a substitute for putting your time in on craft.

If your craft is not strong at the sentence and paragraph level, you'll want to join a writer's workshop (a few $ here and there). Even join several and go iterative - take your work to one group, take on board their improvements and take that improved version to another group, and so on until you have something that reads smooth and easy. Read books on craft like Story Engineering by Larry Brooks (a few $). Maybe take some classes (a few more $).

Next up is Research about Genre. This is where you bend your writing craft to serve the expectations of your readers. Writing great sentences and paragraphs is great, and telling stories is great, but if you can't align to Genre expectation (whether that's Billionaire Romance or Literary Drama or Zombie Apocalypse) you're going to struggle to find readers.

It'd be ideal if you could do your Research before you write word 1 of your novel, but that's unlikely, and it shouldn't be a reason to delay writing anyway. Writing and research can happen at the same time. The Cycle's all about simultaneous learning and improvement.

So you'll write and research, focusing on all the free techniques first as you begin to define your Genre. Look at the top 100 as much as you can bear. Read your comparable authors. I'd recommend buying a K-lytics research pack to get you a jump-start on what you're looking for ($37). Think about where you want to be on the Art-Commerce scale, then think again. If you want to lean toward Art, you're going to have to at least break even on your promotional spend, unless you plan to finance the spread of your books indefinitely.

In sum, you don't need to spend much on the Research stage. Let's say, including some writer's workshop fees, some books, the K-lytics pack and maybe an online craft course, you've spent $100 so far.

Now you're onto Ask. You should be careful here, because you're going to start spending more money. If you've not done enough Research, that money's going to be wasted. I'd recommend you start a 99 Designs contest ($299). This should get you a great, on-Genre cover, which you can poll to various groups as you're working on it with designers. Then I'd start Cycling the body text through beta readers. We haven't got a massive budget, so maybe start with two, let's say $80. Make it clear you want to hear about problems, not only positives.

Depending on what your beta readers say (and especially if they independently point out the same issues), you either move forward or you work to align and get another beta reader to check that. You've got some room in the budget, but not too much - you want to save most of your cash for the ad budget, when you'll get a taste of how your Promise and Delivery align to Genre. If you're concerned about typos, spend another $100 or so on a cheap proofreader off Fiverr, and start using free tools like Grammarly and ProWritingAid.

That takes you up to $559-659 spent so far - various bits of research alongside a K-lytics pack, a 99 Designs, two beta reads and maybe a proofread. You've got $340-440 left, so where do you spend it?

Facebook ads testing out variations of your blurb and ad copy. You can even do this in the pre-publication stage, by sending clicks to your website or newsletter signup or the pre-order page. You've settled on a cover image for now, so you're focusing on getting the best blurb now. If you find one that works well with your audience, they'll likely work well on your sales page too. Publish and try it out. With $340-440 left, you could run $5/day ads for 3 months. That's a good amount of data. A lot of eyes on.

Enough to get you some sales and some reviews, maybe even some data on your readthrough. Look at your numbers and read your reviews. If people start saying the same thing is a problem, you should listen. Dive back into the Cycle and figure out where the problem lies, then work to fix it.

That's the Cycle in a nutshell.

By Element

Cover

- Study top 100 comparable covers
- Outsource cover research to K-lytics
- Read your Reviews
- Ask a Facebook group about your Promise
- Ask a marketing critique group about your Promise
- Poll people you know on your Promise
- Poll the masses on your Promise via Pickfu
- Start a 99 Designs cover contest
- Commission other cover designers
- Sell and analyze via a split test
- Use Facebook ads for testing

Title

- Be inspired by comparable titles
- Outsource title research to K-lytics
- Read your Reviews
- Ask a Facebook group about your Promise

- Ask a marketing critique group about your Promise
- Poll people you know on your Promise
- Poll the masses on your Promise via Pickfu
- Sell and analyze via a split test
- Use Facebook ads for testing

Blurb

- Read your Reviews
- Word cloud analysis of top 100 blurbs
- Overwrite top 100 blurbs
- Write the blurb first
- Read comparable bestsellers
- Use movie classification to define tone
- Ask a Facebook group about your Promise
- Ask a marketing critique group about your Promise
- Poll people you know on your Promise
- Poll the masses on your Promise via Pickfu
- Commission a blurb copywriter
- Sell and analyze via a split test
- Use Facebook ads for testing

Body text

- Read your Reviews
- Read comparable bestsellers
- Use movie classification to define tone
- Poll your fans on your Delivery
- Ask a writer's workshop about your Delivery
- Hire a body text editor

- Cycle through beta readers
- Sell and analyze via a split test

By Pre-publication Status

- Study top 100 comparable covers
- Outsource cover research to K-lytics
- Be inspired by comparable titles
- Outsource title research to K-lytics
- Check comparable prices, formats & KU status
- Word cloud analysis of top 100 blurbs
- Overwrite top 100 blurbs
- Write the blurb first
- Read comparable bestsellers
- Use movie classification to define tone
- Ask a Facebook group about your Promise
- Ask a marketing critique group about your Promise
- Poll people you know on your Promise
- Poll the masses on your Promise via Pickfu
- Start a 99 Designs cover contest
- Commission other cover designers
- Commission a blurb copywriter
- Hire a body text editor
- Cycle through beta readers
- Use Facebook ads for testing

VI. SPIN UP THE FLYWHEEL

NOW WE'VE REACHED the end of the Genre Mastery Cycle, so it's time to recap and reflect. For me, the Cycle started with those 23 books that were losing money or barely breaking even. If my books weren't paying for their promotion, I couldn't get them into the hands of readers, and if I couldn't get them into the hands of readers, what was the point? Was I writing only for myself?

My answer was no. I wanted to reach readers the same way other authors had reached me when I was a kid. I wanted to continue that same relationship from both sides, and if I could make fostering that relationship into my career and income source, so much the better.

So I had to learn to sell.

I started with aligning my covers and blurbs. In time I moved to changing titles and body texts. I came across plenty of techniques to better listen to and harness reader feedback, and gradually pulled myself and my writing into closer alignment with reader expectation.

It's been a real journey. I've talked many times throughout this book about the Cycle throwing up revelations, and it absolutely has. These weren't just revelations about my writing, though, or my readers, but myself too; about how the way I think and act is similar to and different from other people. It's been a journey of self-discovery as much as it's been a journey toward Genre Mastery, and I've enjoyed every minute of it, both the ups and the downs.

It can be the same for you too. This Genre Mastery business, just like writing itself, is a lifelong gig. Genre changes as people and the culture change. To stay on top of it is to know what's going on out there, as well as what's going on inside yourself.

I'm all signed up. I can't think of anything more fascinating than the way we tell each other stories, and how that changes and influences the world.

So let's close things out with the Cycle in action.

I fully intend to practice what I preach when it comes to this book. I've already given several examples of how different stages of the Genre Mastery Cycle caused me to change the book's Promise and Delivery. Very meta. With each change, 'Master Your Genre' grows and gets better.

On that note, I'd love to hear what you think of it and the ideas it contains. So please do let me know:

- Reviews on the shop site where you bought it are one great way.
- Email is another - michaeljohngrist@hotmail.com.
- The Master Your Genre Facebook group's a third - https://www.facebook.com/groups/masteryourgenre

Likewise, if you'd like to share personal examples of how the Cycle has helped you, or if you have any suggestions for techniques to augment the Cycle, those would be inspiring to hear. Perhaps, with your permission, they could be included in future versions of this book. We can all learn so much from the example of others.

If you're looking for more direct Genre Mastery help, advice and suggestions, I offer 1-1 Genre Mastery coaching sessions via my website here - www.michaeljohngrist.com/masteryourgenre/.

Now it's time to put up your sails, light the fuse, rev your engine and get that virtuous circle spinning!

ACKNOWLEDGEMENTS

My deepest thanks and appreciation to:

- Suyoung Lee for her constant support and invaluable suggestions on the earliest draft, and for allowing me to use her excellent book The Tokyo Bicycle Bakery as an example.
- Brad Borkan for extremely useful comments on the graphs, headings and the hook of the opening chapters.
- Patsy Trench for her truly enlightening comments about the Art/Commerce spectrum and this book's position on it, and for helping me to take off some of my brusquer narratorial edges.
- Anette Pollner for her excellent suggestion of the title in an early brainstorm session, and providing her perspective and support on the mid-draft.
- Holly Worton for invaluable suggestions on coping with bad reviews, adding times required for each of the techniques, and the notion of creating a companion workbook.

- Charles Harris for sharing his wisdom on Genre, as well as on the practical consideration of laying out a non-fiction book.
- Kay Seeley for insightfully pointing out I needed a faster start to the book and a definition of Genre right from the off - very true.
- All the members of the London Indie Authors for their support and comradeship on this long and crazy authoring journey.

- Michael

Lightning Source UK Ltd.
Milton Keynes UK
UKHW021019111021
392015UK00014B/1154